Representing Europeans

Representing Europeans

A Pragmatic Approach

Richard Rose
University of Strathclyde, Glasgow

OXFORD
UNIVERSITY PRESS

Great Clarendon Street, Oxford, OX2 6DP,
United Kingdom

Oxford University Press is a department of the University of Oxford.
It furthers the University's objective of excellence in research, scholarship,
and education by publishing worldwide. Oxford is a registered trade mark of
Oxford University Press in the UK and in certain other countries.

British Library Cataloguing in Publication Data
Data available

ISBN 978–0–19–965476–5

Printed by the MPG Printgroup, UK

Contents

Contents

List of Tables

List of Figures

List of Abbreviations/acronyms

ALDE	Alliance of Liberals and Democrats for Europe
CoR	Committee of the Regions
COREPER	Committee of Permanent Representatives
DG	Directorate General
EBRD	European Bank for Reconstruction and Development
ECJ	European Court of Justice
ECB	European Central Bank
ECSC	European Coal and Steel Community
EEC	European Economic Community
EES	European Election Study
EESC	European Economic and Social Committee
EFL	English as a Foreign Language
EFTA	European Free Trade Association
EP	European Parliament
EPP	European People's Party
EU	European Union
MEP	Member of European Parliament
NATO	North Atlantic Treaty Organization
NUT	Territorial Unit of Statistics (from French)
OECD	Organisation of Economic Co-operation and Development
OPEC	Organization of Petroleum Exporting Countries
OSCE	Organization for Security and Co-operation in Europe
PERMREP	Permanent Representative
WTO	World Trade Organization

Every citizen shall have the right to participate in the democratic life of the Union. Decisions shall be taken as openly and as closely as possible to the citizen.

Treaty of the European Union (Maastricht) Article 10.3

Introduction

The End of Integration by Stealth

The tragic events we have lived through have perhaps made us wiser. But men pass on and others take their place. We will not be able to hand on our personal experience. It will die with us. What we can hand on are institutions.

Jean Monnet

We have reached a stage where the political agenda can no longer hide behind the economic one, and must assert itself in its own right. These issues cannot be dealt with if Europe remains an UPO—an Unidentified Political Object.

Jacques Delors, President, European Commission 2001

The European Union was not created by pressures from public opinion to represent 'We the People of Europe'. The treaties that serve as the EU's constitution have been negotiated by European officials and national governments with virtually no public involvement. In accordance with the normal practice of international law, treaties are signed by heads of state. Popular participation is not considered necessary. Thus, the Treaty on European Union declares that it is adopted in the name of His Majesty the King of the Belgians, followed by a succession of presidents and monarchs that concludes with the commitment of Her Majesty the Queen of the United Kingdom of Great Britain and Northern Ireland.

The founders of the European Union thought first of Europe rather than Europeans.[1] A legacy of war and depression had shown the failure of the historic European system of sovereign states. The goal was to escape the evils of Europe's past by creating new institutions that would secure freedom, peace, and prosperity through the development of an ever closer Union. The European Coal and Steel Community took economic resources essential for war out of the hands of national governments and created a supra-national European Commission to carry out policies binding on national governments. The 1957 Treaty of Rome created the European Economic Community.

The architect who designed the initial European institutions, Jean Monnet, envisioned European integration as advancing by stealth. He did not emulate Winston Churchill in making grand proclamations about European values. Instead, Monnet operated behind the scenes to create institutions that would, almost unnoticed, adopt seemingly small economic measures that demonstrated the practical benefits of European integration. Instead of having an electoral mandate, the European Commission was created to develop effective policies that would have little political visibility, but would cumulatively promote European integration. In the words of Walter Hallstein, the first chair of the European Commission, 'The Communities are in politics, not business.' The strategy of integration by stealth was designed to lead eventually to a United States of Europe.[2]

The benefits of European integration have been transformed in half a century. The means by which Napoleon and Hitler sought to unify Europe, described by Winston Churchill as 'war, war', has been replaced by 'jaw, jaw', in which leaders of national governments meeting in the European Council, Members of the European Parliament, and European Commission civil servants talk through policies promoting European integration. EU leaders have claimed credit for economic growth that by the end of the twentieth century gave ordinary Europeans a standard of living far beyond anything that could have been imagined by the EU's founders.

The impact of EU policies has been transformed too. As long as the benefits are large and costs low, or at least not visible, the European Union could operate as an Unidentified Political Object. The absence of public interest could be interpreted as showing that it did so with the 'permissive consensus' of Europeans.[3] However, the Eurozone crisis has resulted in visible costs coming before distant benefits and awakened public opinion. Instead of being asleep, it is now an elephant, poking its nose into what is done in Brussels and what Brussels does to it.

European Union policymakers have responded to the crisis of the Eurozone with a call for more of the same, that is, to increase political integration. The President of the Commission, José Manuel Barroso, has invoked Jean Monnet's dream of a federal Europe as the only way to end Europe's crisis of confidence and compete with the superpowers of a globalized world.

> A deep and genuine economic and monetary union, a political union with a coherent foreign and defence policy, means ultimately that the present European Union must evolve. And let us not be afraid of the words. We will need to move toward a federation of nation states.[4]

This prescription ignores the public debate about whether the European Union is part of the problem or part of the solution. This book adopts a twenty-first century approach. It argues that the end of integration by stealth requires the European Union to secure the political commitment of people who are both national and EU citizens.

I The Need for Popular Commitment

To charge the EU with having a democratic deficit on the grounds that it ought to be governed like a democratic state is a category error; it confuses the relation of states with each other and the relation between individual citizens and their state. The United Nations and the International Monetary Fund show that major intergovernmental institutions are neither democratic nor are most of their member states democratic. The EU is a Unique Political Object because it is an intergovernmental organization that requires its member states to be democracies.

In 1992 the EU's Maastricht Treaty conferred European citizenship on everyone who was already a citizen of a member state. However, when a Eurobarometer survey asked European citizens what was meant by the term citizen of Europe, a majority said that they didn't know. Only 43 per cent of people on whom citizenship has been automatically conferred claim to have an idea of what this means. Even more tellingly, only 33 per cent think that their voice counts in the EU.[5]

There is a sharp contrast between the influence that individuals have on national governments and the very restricted influence that the same people have on the governance of the European Union. The EU's governors are not accountable, as is the case in a democratic political system, because European citizens cannot vote for a European government nor can they vote it out of office. As national citizens, people have the right to challenge their government about what it does in Brussels; however, as European citizens they do not have the right to challenge what is collectively adopted there. The absence of influence encourages a lack of commitment to the policies that the EU adopts.

The argument. The European Union needs the commitment of its citizens in order to deal with the problems that today challenge Europeans on a continental scale. Justifying more integration by invoking achievements of a half century ago has no more appeal than a black-and-white television set. Europeans today have a very different experience of politics than their grandparents. They are not haunted by the fear of armed invasion nor are they deferential or trusting of their governors.

Instead of engaging in a discussion about what democracy means in the abstract, this book focuses on what the shortfall in popular commitment means for the European Union. It asks first: Who or what do European Union institutions represent? The short answer is: Most don't represent people; they represent other organizations or abstract principles. Secondly:

How, if at all, do Europe's citizens relate to EU institutions? The answer is: Indirectly or not at all. Given weak links between Europe's citizens and policymakers, what is the best way to find out whether agreements made in Brussels to advance an ever closer Union actually represent the views of their citizens? The answer is: The commitment of citizens to further transfers of powers to Brussels can best be tested by a pan-European referendum.

The idea of directly consulting Europe's citizens is rejected by most EU policymakers. In the tradition of Jean Monnet, they see themselves as trustees acting for the collective good of Europe. Insofar as the creation of an ever closer Union is regarded as of overriding political importance, then popular politics should be kept out of deciding the future of Europe. Decisions should be taken by a consensus among EU policymakers. However, consensus at the European level introduces a double distortion. First of all, it assumes that when prime ministers make commitments in the name of their country they speak for all of their citizens. Public opinion surveys show that they do not. Secondly, a consensus among 27 national governments can only be arrived at by compromises that leave each with a curate's egg that is good and bad in parts.

Any referendum will reveal a division of opinion about what is agreed in Brussels. A referendum creates a fear among policymakers that their decisions will be rejected by citizens whom they nominally represent. Rather than allaying their fears by campaigning for popular support for an ever closer Union, policymakers reject measures to give citizens more voice. The evidence that follows shows that their fear is often mistaken.

Does it matter? In an age of 24/7 globalization, the boundaries between nation-states have become increasingly porous. Many problems facing national governments—financing deficits, promoting trade, or combatting terrorism—are not confined within national boundaries. Interdependence is a visible fact of life in big countries such as Britain and Germany as well as in small countries with big neighbours, such as Ireland and Austria. In dealing with problems of interdependence, no national government can completely control what happens to it. This is good reason for collective EU action.

When collective action imposes visible costs, as in the Eurozone crisis, national governments are pulled in opposing directions by the need to reconcile competing national and European demands. They are simultaneously accountable to their national electorate and parliament while in meetings in Brussels they are under pressure to accept decisions that represent a consensus of 27 national governments. There is a trade-off for national governments between accepting measures that are good for Europe as a whole and opposing their adoption in response to national opinion. In an increasingly interdependent world, the politics of Europe is about tension management.

National governments face complementary risks. Measures decided in Brussels may succeed in imposing costs on many member states without securing the promised benefits. Alternatively, if the EU is unable to act effectively, then what happens will be decided on other continents. Clinging to outmoded concepts of national sovereignty can keep the formal right of decisionmaking in national hands but as and when the mace of sovereignty is wielded it will be shattered by stronger forces. Thus, even though the British government increasingly seeks to opt out of EU decisions, it cannot opt out of the effect of what happens in an international economy in which Eurozone countries have a larger displacement than the United Kingdom.

Popular commitment is needed if the EU is to carry out effective policies that have costs as well as benefits, such as measures to resolve the Eurozone crisis. Otherwise, agreements arrived at by elites risk repudiation by national electorates when their costs are known. The fear of public opinion has encouraged a 'too little, too late' approach to policy. In the words of the veteran Eurozone prime minister, Jean-Claude Juncker, 'We all know what to do, but we don't know how to get re-elected once we have done it.'

The European Union has yet to find the means of securing popular commitment to measures agreed at the EU level but subject to challenge nationally. The EU offers citizenship lite: the rights that an individual has as a citizen of Europe are fewer than their rights as national citizens; so too are the obligations. It is complemented by commitment lite to EU institutions. The EU's own Eurobarometer surveys show that half of Europe's citizens are not interested in what the EU does. This is not surprising, since the EU's work is conducted in a distant country and language foreign to most EU citizens. A lack of interest in EU affairs is compounded by limited popular understanding of EU institutions and less media attention to the activities of the European Union than to European Cup football competition. Defenders of the EU system argue that uninformed and uninterested people are unsuited to taking decisions on major EU matters. This ignores the argument in favour of democratic participation: bringing people into the political process is a good way to gain commitment to what governors do.

It is an oversimplification to divide the peoples of Europe into two categories, those who are for and those against the European Union, and it is even more misleading to polarize people into supporters of a united Europe and those wanting their country to withdraw from the EU. There are moderate positions between these two extremes. Among committed supporters of European integration, fundamentalists who advocate European unity as an ideal are now outnumbered by Euro-realists, who want to use the opportunities that existing EU institutions offer to promote policies for collective action that have substantial support among European-level interests. The subtext of these activities is furnished by Jean Monnet: this is the practical way of advancing an ever closer Union.

The label Eurosceptic is confusingly applied to different kinds of unwilling EU citizens. People can accept the existing powers of Brussels as a fait accompli yet disapprove of measures to extend its powers on the grounds that 'small is beautiful' or having greater trust in the actions of their own national institutions. They are soft eurosceptics. The British Conservative government is notable for having many MPs who are hard eurosceptics. They are actively pushing for the return to Westminster of a significant number of powers that have been transferred to the EU or to withdraw from the European Union.

The balance of public opinion rests with people who have no fixed commitment for or against the goal of an ever closer European Union. Uncommitted Europeans are numerous enough to tip popular support for or against policies advancing European integration. Some are of two minds about what the EU is doing, approving the single Europe market while opposing big EU subsidies for agriculture, or approving EU measures for social protection while opposing the competition that accompanies the single market. Others have no opinion, answering 'don't know' to Eurobarometer polls. As long as people are unaware of being European citizens, then under-commitment is of no political consequence. However, EU laws and regulations that now fill more than 90,000 pages and grow bulkier every year are increasingly reminding people that even if you are not interested in what the European Union does, it is interested in what you do.

The pragmatic approach of this book is questioning rather than committed to a view that the EU is always right or that it is always wrong. It rejects commitment to an ever closer Union as an end in itself, the implicit or explicit assumption of many studies of European integration. Pragmatism is consistent with scepticism in the original Greek sense: it encourages asking questions and searching for evidence before coming to a conclusion. The answer arrived at may or may not endorse a policy that increases European integration. It reflects David Hume's Enlightenment principle of testing ideas against experience. After more than half a century, there is lots of experience about the ways in which EU institutions do and do not represent Europeans.

Pragmatism evaluates existing policies by asking how they work and what their consequences are. When there is political dissatisfaction in a given policy area, pragmatists first diagnose the causes of the problem without any commitment for or against EU action. This is more open-minded than the Community method, which assumes that the European Union is best suited to deal with every major problem facing national governments. In a world of interdependence, there are many collective action problems that could justify EU engagement, but that is no guarantee that the EU has the capacity to act effectively. Thus, instead of debating what the EU ought to do about such things as the failure of European economies to converge, the pragmatist first asks: What *can* the European Union do? This avoids the mistake of confusing exhortation with effective action. Does a proposed policy address the causes of a problem? How will it operate? What political and administrative resources are required to achieve its aims? If these pragmatic criteria are met, then the adoption of a measure can be debated on the grounds of its political desirability. In such circumstances, pragmatism may support effective steps towards an ever closer Union. However, if a proposal fails to meet pragmatic criteria, there is a *prima facie* case for going back to the drawing board to match means and ends to deal with a problem, while national governments meanwhile show how effectively or ineffectively they can act without direction from the European Commission.

While this book respects the benefits that integration has brought, its pragmatic approach questions the assumption of the desirability of more of the same, that is, the classic Community method of adopting one-size-fits-all policies for the varied problems now confronting 27 diverse member states and their peoples. Instead, it proposes a look-before-you-leap approach to evaluating EU policies pragmatically.

II A Bridge Too Far?

European integration has two meanings, one static and the other dynamic. Its weaker form is a description of the European Union as it is today; integration describes the institutional system within which member states carry out common policies. While this description is accurate as far as it goes, it doesn't go far enough. It fails to take into account the dynamics that have turned an institution with six member states and very limited powers into a Union with significant powers over 27 member states and a readiness to acquire more powers. A static description assumes that the EU operates in a stable environment. The appearance of stability, described by critics as stagnation, occurs only when member states are not faced with challenges. This is anything but the case today. For EU policymakers to do nothing today would be an admission that the issues for which it is responsible are out of control.

Where the European Union stands today is the dynamic consequence of past decisions. In dynamic terms European integration is a process of moving toward an ever closer Union of European states. A bicycling metaphor is sometimes used to describe the need for continuous movement. If a steady forward momentum, involving the deepening and broadening of policies, does not occur, there is a risk of collapse. However, the idea that movement is desirable depends on the direction that is being taken. Critics pay unintended tribute to the strength of the EU's momentum by claiming that European integration has gone too far. In the sardonic words of one, 'The fact that the EU is not perfect does not mean it cannot get worse'.[6]

7

If this book had been written a decade ago, it would have focused on the challenge of enlarging the European Union to incorporate ten new member states from Eastern Europe. Ten years is a short span of time but a long way from where the European Union finds itself today. The EU now faces major challenges to its economic and political foundations. It is over-reacting to see the Eurozone crisis as evidence of the EU breaking up. However, it is under-reacting to ignore changes in the political debate about the future of Europe. Events have demonstrated that while central banks and economists claim to be apolitical, politics and economics are inextricably linked in the governance of Europe and in the EU's impact on the lives of its citizens.

The immediate challenges that the European Union now faces come from within the ranks of older member states. Ireland, Portugal, and Greece, the three most troubled Eurozone countries, have each belonged to the EU for more than a quarter of a century. Another vulnerable country, Italy, was a founder member of the European Union. The historic anchors, Germany and France, face challenges radically different from the 1950s. Moreover, the British view of EU membership is no longer what it was in 1975, when 64 per cent endorsed EU membership in a referendum. Given that so many facts have changed, Keynes's injunction to think afresh is apt.

The technocratic justification for creating the European Central Bank, which was modelled on the German *Bundesbank*, was that it would enable all Eurozone countries to achieve high growth and low inflation. The executive board of the European Central Bank (ECB) consists, according to its charter, of 'persons of recognised standing and professional experience in monetary or banking matters' and a Governing Council of members of national central banks in the Eurozone. Locating its headquarters in Frankfurt am Main emphasized its independence of Brussels and commitment to Germany's tradition of giving priority to fighting inflation. The technical complexities of the ECB's operation are well beyond the understanding of most of the policymakers who approved it; it makes decisions by stealth with a substantial political impact. In the words of the European Council President, the introduction of the euro implied the need for a full-fledged economic and political union: 'However, the general public was not really made aware of it.'[7] The political implications of a single currency made Britain, Denmark, and Sweden stay out of the Eurozone when it came into effect.

The Eurozone crisis shows the risk of going a bridge too far; a single currency was adopted to further European integration among ill-matched countries in an institution with inadequate powers.[8] Now that the euro has come under heavy fire in international financial markets, it cannot be abandoned as readily as an unsuccessful military attempt to seize a strategic bridge. The official doctrine is that national membership in the Eurozone is irreversible.

Governments of both lender and debtor states are pulled in opposing directions by European institutions and national electorates. National governments are expected to comply with recommendations of EU institutions to reduce their deficits immediately by reducing public spending, the bulk of which goes on pensions, health care, and education. The nationally popular alternative is to stimulate growth in the economy by the Keynesian policy of increased public spending. However, indebted governments do not have the money to spend, they face punitive interest rates to finance the cost of past debts, and, as Eurozone members, they lack the ability to print money.

Indebted Mediterranean states appear weak because they have difficulty in borrowing the money they need to meet current obligations arising from past borrowings and to finance current expenditure. However, lenders are vulnerable because if these debts are not repaid their own balance sheets would be filled with red ink and some banks would be at risk of bankruptcy. Before the euro was introduced, debtors could ease their position by devaluing their currency, a strategy Sweden and Britain have used more than once. Eurozone countries cannot do so, short of leaving the Eurozone. This would not only create fresh domestic difficulties but also call into question the maintenance of the Eurozone as an engine for European integration, as well as source of funds for indebted member states.

The EU is seeking to maintain the Eurozone by a strategy that the French describe as *la fuite en avant*, that is, running away forwards. The plan is to get rid of the threat that indebted countries pose to the future of the EU's integrated currency by loaning more money to indebted countries with strict conditions attached. These conditions are set out in the 2012 Treaty on Stability, Coordination, and Governance agreed by 25 member states; Britain and the Czech Republic are the outsiders. National budgets are expected to have a structural deficit of no more than one-half of one per cent. A government can be subjected to fines of hundreds of millions or billions of euros if Brussels decides that it has failed to meet this target and fines can be enforced by a binding decision of the European Court of Justice. In an English understatement, a lawyer comments, 'This is unlikely to generate inter-state harmony between the 25 signatories.'[9] Moreover, the Treaty's conditions are meant to be applied not only in small states such as Greece, Ireland, and Portugal, but also in big states with a much greater political and economic displacement, such as Spain, Italy, and France.

Working on the hypothesis that cash begets control, the EU has made an open-ended pledge to buy short-term bonds of countries whose governments meet its conditions. These include reductions of spending and raising taxes in accord with balanced budget principles; abandoning lax regulatory and spending policies that benefited political supporters but not the economy; and raising standards of governance to reduce waste and corruption. In addition, countries are being pushed to take actions to increase their competitiveness internationally, since they cannot do so by devaluing their currency. The EU and the International Monetary Fund will supervise the implementation of reforms. The EU has not done so before because, as a senior ECB official has noted, 'When you deal with banks, you deal with politics. Automatically. It's very dangerous'.[10]

The amount of cash available to indebted countries depends on decisions taken in lending states as well as in Brussels. The funds available are provided by national governments and national parliaments now have MPs asking questions that are awkward because they raise legitimate doubts about how and whether new measures can be effectively implemented. The German Federal Court has ruled that payment additional to its 190bn commitment of euros must be approved by the German Parliament, which faces re-election in October 2013. The conditions are also subject to supervision by the German Federal Court in Karlsruhe, and it has mandated that German participants in Eurozone decisions keep MPs informed of ongoing discussions so that in an emergency the Parliament is not confronted with a fait accompli.

If a borrowing country fails to meet the ECB's conditions then the ECB can either give the debtor an open-ended commitment in terms of the time required to pay back its debts or stop buying its bonds and threaten the country's exit from the Eurozone, with uncertain consequences for its remaining members, both lenders and borrowers.

However, measures justified at the EU level as economically necessary to save the Eurozone can be challenged as politically unacceptable at the national level. National citizens can use their votes to eject from office a government that is squeezing pensions, raising taxes, and imposing visible, immediate, and harsh economic costs to meet EU directives. However, changing control of a national government does not get rid of the pressures that it faces from Brussels and from international financial markets.

The debate about what to do to save the Eurozone has gone public because the measures recommended have big and visible costs. Public reaction shows that nationalism is not dead but transformed. The traditional definition of a nation—the territory that a group of people would fight and die for—is no longer relevant. In Europe today a nation can be defined by economics: it is a group of people who are willing to pay taxes to resolve the financial problems of others. This willingness stops at the national border. The resistance to transfer payments is found not only in Germany but also among Greeks and Spaniards who do not want to pay national taxes so that their government can use the money to repay debts incurred in the past to foreign institutions. In short, the Eurozone has created a common currency but not a single nation for the purposes of paying taxes.

III Diagnosis and Prescription

The first chapter shows how the EU political system institutionalizes two essential features of democratic politics. Its diverse institutions are representative of a plurality of states, interests, peoples, and principles and there is lots of accountability, since its institutions impose many checks and balances on each other. This prevents any one country or institution from dominating the EU; instead, decisions require bargaining to arrive at a consensus. However, weak links between EU decisionmakers and Europe's citizens mean that citizens have limited commitment and trust in the EU's institutions. Explaining how the EU works today by citing treaties signed in the distant past by long dead politicians is insufficient to secure popular commitment. Nor can justification of EU institutions on grounds of effectiveness, such as the EU's historic promotion of economic growth, deliver popular commitment when the European economy falters.

Although the European Union's scope was limited when it started, there was no limit on ambitions. The dynamic that has forged today's ever closer Union is set out in Chapter 2. Big bang treaties agreed between member states have given the EU new powers. Concurrently, quiet discussions in Brussels have maintained the momentum for adopting many seemingly small laws and regulations that cumulatively affect Europeans in big ways. The EU's power to have a direct effect on citizens is limited because it lacks the money and public employees of member states. However, it compensates by exercising lawmaking powers superior to those of national governments. While the EU's appetite for integration has grown with its institutions, that of Europe's citizens has not.

The refusal to place boundaries on the definition of Europe makes the European Union open to a diversity of peoples. Chapter 3 documents how the fall of the Berlin Wall has been followed by the EU more than doubling its membership. This has not only changed the EU's size but also its shape. The EU now includes countries whose Atlantic coastlines link them to Boston and Brazil and countries whose eastern boundaries are with Russia and Turkey. Its members differ greatly in population and income, and in corruption too. Concurrently, television, travel, and work have exposed people to influences from other countries. However, contrary to expectations, Europeanization has not created a demand for more European integration.

The European Union is open to discussing policies with a multiplicity of multi-national institutions. In the Council national governments are under pressure to agree compromises with more than two dozen other national governments and defend agreements to their national electorates. The European Commission and European Parliament are continuously in discussion with trans-national organizations advancing claims in the name of business, industry, and civil society. Efforts to reach beyond organizations based in Brussels encounter both practical and political difficulties. The constitutional convention that the EU called did not have any input from its citizens. Chapter 4 shows that the result is citizenship lite.

Referendums enable citizens to participate directly in politics but EU policy-makers reject this institution of direct democracy as inconsistent with their definition of direct democracy. Referendums also pose a risk to their power to commit EU citizens to decisions that they take as trustees on their behalf. By contrast, a clear majority of European citizens want the right to vote in referendums deciding whether more major steps should be taken towards an ever closer Union. Member states have called dozens of national referendums on measures expanding the EU's constitutional powers. Chapter 5 shows that even when a majority endorses further European integration, each referendum vote shows more division among citizens than appears from the consensus decisions of EU institutions. Furthermore, almost one-quarter have rejected decisions agreed in Brussels.

Europe's citizens do have the right to elect Members of the European Parliament (MEPs). However, the Parliament is not elected on the basis of one person, one vote, one value. Instead, seats are assigned to member states by a formula of degressive proportionality. A better name for this formula is disproportional representation; the number of MEPs assigned to smaller countries is much bigger than their share of the European population would justify. Chapter 6 shows that the EP gives unequal representation to the citizens of Europe. Moreover, there is an asymmetry of representation; a majority of electors do not bother to vote for an MEP, while MEPs work hard to advance policies in Brussels with little contact with the electors they nominally represent.

To participate effectively in the European Parliament's activities, MEPs representing more than 160 national parties join multi-national European Party Groups. Nominally, the Groups endorse socialist, liberal, green or vague popular principles. Whatever policy commitments are given in the national programmes on which MEPs are elected, MEPs usually vote along lines laid down by the whip of their multi-national Group. In most cases the majority is formed by MEPs from the Socialist and People's Party Groups. However, Chapter 7 shows that these are the two Groups whose MEPs have disagreed most in the programmes that they present to their national voters. The effect of such co-operation is that the European Parliament is a cartel advancing European integration.

In peace as in war states no longer enjoy stand-alone sovereignty. The interdependence of policies across national boundaries results in national governments lacking the full capacity to make effective policies; outcomes are the result of decisions of other countries as well as their own. A primary justification of the European Union is that it adopts collective policies that deal with the challenge of interdependence in such trans-national fields as trade and environmental pollution. Chapter 8 shows how the increase in interdependent issues has resulted in policy changing politics. But politics also affects policy, when there is no consensus about what the EU ought to do. The Eurozone crisis is a striking example: it forces Germans to worry about Greek financial policies and Greeks to worry about the standards that the German government sets for public finance. Globalization gives the single Europe market an international dimension while simultaneously exposing it to influences beyond the control of Brussels. To deny the reality of interdependence is to pursue a foreign policy without foreigners.

Interdependence stimulates demands for collective action but it does not guarantee that the European Union has the capacity to supply a solution. Chapter 9 identifies major deficits in the EU's capacity to act. These include legal challenges from the German Federal Court and the British Parliament, and the lack of money to meet the potential financial claims of the Eurozone crisis. The EU also lacks the power to maintain the rule of law in old member states where corruption is chronic, as well as in new member states where corruption has remained high since their admission. The EU's lack of capacity should place limits on enlargement, when seven of the eight countries that are now potential candidates for admission have far weaker economies and more corruption than member states. The varying characteristics of 27 member states make the EU today a political system in which diversity is the norm. This reduces the likelihood that one-size-fits-all policies will produce benefits clearly outweighing costs for every member state. When disagreements arise about what the EU should do, the alternatives are for the EU to do nothing or for member states that want to form coalitions of the willing to do so. The EU has procedures for enhanced co-operation that enable countries favouring steps towards an ever closer Union to act together while the unwilling stand aside and watch what happens to those who go first. The Eurozone is an example of this.

The conclusion argues that giving all of Europe's citizens a chance to register their views in pan-European referendums on EU treaties would be the best way to test how much popular commitment there is to the expansion of EU powers. It would also be fairer, getting rid of the current practice of one nation, whether small, like Ireland, or large, like Britain, calling a referendum that vetoes a treaty signed by 27 governments. If national governments do represent their citizens in multi-national Brussels deliberations, in the great majority of states a referendum will endorse what their governors have done and losers should accept defeat in a national referendum. If there are countries where a majority is against a treaty, then procedures for enhanced co-operation should allow it to opt out. The majority can demonstrate what the benefits of such a step may be while others await evidence on which to make a pragmatic decision about whether the benefits are worth the costs. A successful policy would encourage countries that initially opted out to join subsequently in order to share the benefits of integration. This was the basis on which the United Kingdom joined the European Union a decade and one-half after initially refusing to be a founder. An unsuccessful policy would confirm the view of member states that opted out that some steps towards an ever closer Union are better avoided. Events have produced a British consensus that it was desirable not to be a founder member of the Eurozone.

IV Perspective of the Author

The European Union is valuable because many problems of interdependence cannot be effectively dealt with by states acting in isolation. Small European states, a big majority of the members of the European Union, have long known this. The logic of European Union action can often be defended by a motto of an unwilling EU citizen, Margaret Thatcher, 'There is no alternative.' However, this book is critical of the way in which half a billion people have had to accept an unending series of moves towards an ever closer Union without the right to check major Brussels decisions and say 'Enough is enough.' Pan-European referendums would provide this. While the voice of the people is not always right, it is wrong to deny citizens any say in making crucial decisions about how they and their children will be governed for generations in the future. That is why this book gives two not three cheers for the European Union as it is today.

Because the European Union encompasses diverse peoples, the book's audience is diverse. It is addressed to everyone who is familiar with English, whether as a native English or American speaker or knowing English as a Foreign Language (EFL). EFL is the language of political discourse in the European Union today. EFL-speakers do not think that a market is best defined by an absence of controls. The fact that Britain is governed by native English-speakers is a problem for both London and Brussels. EFL-speakers can also be a problem for Washington, where Europe tends to be seen as a junior partner in NATO, an assumption that is challenged by European states that do not contribute manpower or money to US-led initiatives on other continents.

This book is a work of political science in the traditional sense of politics being about the exercise of power, and science about acquiring knowledge through the systematic observation and interpretation of evidence rather than by introspection, abstraction, or assertion. It cites public opinion surveys showing divisions about Europe in order to reject the methodological nationalism that assumes national governments represent all their citizens when participating in EU decisionmaking. This evidence also undermines the assumption of EU treaties reflecting a common will of Europeans.

To communicate what is important about the European Union, I give clarity precedence over professional jargon. If some readers regard vivid phrasing as provocative, this is better than hiding political controversy under a blanket of abstractions and qualifications. Because this book covers a wide ground, it draws on a large and diverse range of academic writings about European Union institutions that have been helpful in formulating an argument that sometimes significantly challenges the conventional wisdom found there. Since many readers concerned with European affairs have neither the free access to journals in university libraries nor the training required to follow statistical analyses that proliferate there, footnotes are restricted to sources of direct quotations. An appendix provides a note on further reading.

The distinctive approach of this book reflects my own scholarly background in the study of public opinion and of presidents and prime ministers. This has given me sympathy with people at the top and people at the bottom of the multiple political systems in which Europe's elites and citizens are now embedded. At one time or another I have presented my ideas in seminars and lectures in 25 of the 27 member states of the European Union and in publications translated into 11 European languages.

I am a European but not a European citizen. Having dual citizenship in the state of Missouri as well as the United States has helped me to understand multi-level government and an American upbringing has certainly made it easier to see Europe as a whole. Having started studies in Europe when the legacy of war was very evident in cathedrals without roofs and men without an arm or a leg, I have a deep respect for the founders of the European Union, who had seen much more and much worse. That era, fortunately, is now past. Final alterations to the text were made in autumn 2012, when the EU's policy-makers hoped that they had arrived at a means of turning the Eurozone crisis into an opportunity for further European integration, but their hopes had yet to be tested by the pressure of events.

Funding for the research reported here has come primarily from the British Economic and Social Research Council grant RES-062-23-1892. It has been augmented by a grant from the Fundação Manuel dos Santos, Lisbon to the Robert Schuman Centre of the European University Institute, Florence. Findings from this book have been presented in academic seminars and conferences in seven European countries and the United States. Technical discussion and evidence are contained in journal articles and chapters of edited books. I have benefited from the research assistance of Dr Gabriela Borz and from collaboration in writing papers with her and with Professor Patrick Bernhagen, now of Zeppelin University, both true Europeans in their formation and interests.

I have also benefited from many conversations in Brussels with officials of the European Council, the European Commission, the European Parliament, representatives of national governments, and think tanks. Useful comments and challenges to the work in progress have been made by Graham Avery, Daniela Corona, Laura Cram, Richard Corbett, Wilhelm Lehmann, Christopher Lord, and Frank Vibert. The argument and errors are my own.

1

The EU System: Accountable Up to a Point

Institutions, adequately structured, can accumulate and transmit the wisdom of successive generations.

Jean Monnet

The Union shall have an institutional framework which shall aim to promote its values, advance its objectives, serve its interests, those of its citizens and those of the member states.

Treaty of the European Union, Article 13.1

Representation, accountability and the sanction of elections are essential elements of a democratic political system. The political system of each EU member state meets all these criteria. Political parties, MPs, interest groups and diverse institutions represent the views found in free societies; the government of the day is accountable to parliament; and if citizens are dissatisfied with how their government has represented them, they can turn it out of office with their votes. The European Union meets two of these three criteria.

The European Union has representative institutions. The European Parliament is directly elected to represent the citizens of its 27 member states and the national governments that represent the states in the EU's decisionmaking councils are elected too. Interest groups represent the interests of important economic sectors of society. Judges represent legal principles and the European Central Bank represents principles of experts in the so-called dismal science of economics. The variety of non-elected EU institutions reflects the fact that 'both the concept and the practice of representation have had little to do with democracy or liberty'.[1]

The checks and balances of the EU system institutionalize horizontal accountability. Policymakers in each institution are obliged to inform, explain and justify their actions to other institutions in the system. Accountability is hard if an institution has the power to stop a policy from being enacted. It is soft when an institution can be questioned but the questioners lack the power to stop them from acting; this is the status of many EU advisory bodies. To arrive at a decision requires a consensus achieved by bargaining between representatives of a combination of EU institutions. The EU's co-decision rules give both the Council, representing the national governments of member states, and the European Parliament, representing citizens, the power to reject legislative proposals of the supra-national European Commission. Some non-elected institutions have hard sanctions too; for example, the Court of Justice of the European Union can void the actions of other institutions. The EU's horizontal system of checks and balances is consistent with pre-democratic ideas of balanced government expressed by ancient Greek authors such as Polybius, and with the separation of powers doctrine of Montesquieu.

Vertical sanctions are weak. The system thus gives a distinctive twist to the saying of an American Member of Congress—'all politics is local'; the locale of its politics is Brussels. EU institutions exercising checks and balances are within walking distance of each other. Horizontal accountability is no substitute for the third requirement of democracy—the vertical accountability of governors to governed. The EU system does not give European citizens what the political theorist Robert Dahl describes as essential for democracy, 'The people must have the final say'.[2] Citizens do not have the hard power to vote the EU's government out of office.

The Treaty of the European Union emphasizes the first priority of EU institutions as representing the values, objectives, and interests of the Union itself. The supra-national European Commission is able to do so since EU treaties make it the sole source of legislative and policy proposals. The institutions of the European Union have not been designed to promote democratic participation but to facilitate the momentum of an ever closer Union. Expanding the scope for consensus by taking the opinion of European citizens into account would increase vertical accountability. However, it would slow down progress towards an ever closer Union.

Many European citizens do not share the enthusiasm of the European Commission for the Community method, which favours it taking the initiative when countries face problems. When the 2009 European Election Study asked which level of government deals with the most important problem facing their country, an absolute majority saw their national government as most important and only one-third the EU. When people were then asked who ought to deal with the most important problem facing their country, the answer was the same: 52 per cent wanted their national government to handle it and only one-third favoured European institutions doing so.

1 What EU Institutions Represent

The European Union does not have a constitution in the conventional meaning of the term, a single document that sets out who has constituted it and why. It does, however, have a political system created by a series of treaties that set out its institutions, procedures, and powers. The plural term 'powers' is a literal translation of the French *les pouvoirs*, activities that an institution is legally authorized to undertake. These powers can also be described as its legal competences. This does not mean that EU institutions are always competent, that is, capable of making effective use of their formal powers. Nonetheless, the impact of EU powers is felt whether they are exercised competently or not.

The Lisbon Treaty declares that the European Union is a representative democracy; however, it does not define what this term means. The simplest and most literal definition of representation is that it makes present what is absent. In the EU small member states, absent from informal summit meetings of world leaders, have the same right to be present in EU deliberations as member states with more than one hundred times their population. A second definition is that representatives speak on behalf of those whom they claim to represent. But this leaves open the medieval issue of *quo warranto*, that is, by what right do you claim to represent others? While both national governments and MEPs can claim that election justifies their speaking for Europe's citizens, they are elected in very different ways—and many institutions, such as the Court of Justice and the European Central Bank, represent principles rather than people.

Representative institutions are a lot older than democracy. Many monarchs claimed to represent the whole of society in their own person. The modern state developed as an institution that could make demands on people who were its subjects rather than as an institution that was expected to be responsive to popular wants. For most of its history, the British Parliament represented a hereditary nobility and land-owning interests with a material stake in society. Such representatives were not accountable to a mass electorate. The eighteenth-century MP Edmund Burke argued that MPs ought to be trustees defining and advancing the interests of those whom they nominally represented. The founders of the European Union saw themselves as trustees for the wellbeing of Europe as a whole.

The European Union is often discussed as if it were a single institution, as in the phrase 'Brussels has decided.' In fact, the institutions concentrated in Brussels form a complicated system of institutions that differ in their functions and in what they represent. In the abstract, the functions of EU institutions appear broadly similar to those of member states, such as formulating policies, regulating the market, and resolving legal conflicts. However, because the EU is a multi-national organization representing governments, citizens, and interests from 27 states plus supra-national EU interests, it is different in kind from national counterparts. For example, in the European Council, where heads of national governments meet, a prime minister is not first among equals. Instead, she or he is one among 27 heads of national governments.

Institutions combine constituencies and functions. Politics unites what institutions divide. The European Union has a mixed system of government. The mix includes the European Commission, which represents the ideal of a supra-national Union; the European Council representing national governments; the popularly elected European Parliament; and the Court of Justice. Checks can be applied by national governments, officials of the European Commission, the European Parliament or the Court of Justice. The EU's combination of small and large member states adds another dimension to the mix. Within the EU, small states can check the power of big states thanks to rules requiring super-majorities or unanimity and big states can reduce the influence of the EU's highest offices over themselves by having these offices occupied by politicians from small states.

The *European Council* is the EU institution in which national governments sit; each is represented by a prime minister whose predecessor signed the treaty that committed the country to EU membership. Council members have two contrasting constituencies. As heads of democratically elected governments, they are accountable to their national electorates, who judge them by their performance in national politics. In the Council, prime ministers are one of a group of heads of member states who are expected to adopt a *communautaire* perspective that gives European interests substantial weight. Because no country is big enough to dominate the European Council, a national government must be prepared to make concessions to European claims in order to obtain national concessions in exchange. To treat the Council as simply an arena for fighting for national interests, as British prime ministers have been inclined to do, can win headlines in the London press but lose potential allies in the European Council.

The Lisbon Treaty (Article 15.1) defines the chief function of the European Council as determining the general political direction and priorities of the European Union. Because its members are busy heads of national governments, Council discussions can focus only on big issues. Some of these issues concern the long-term development of an ever closer Union, while others are fire-fighting responses to emergencies for which the EU has direct responsibilities, such as the Eurozone. When big issues concern international crises that the EU has little capacity to influence, the Council can issue a statement calling, for example, for peace in the Middle East. The European Council has the authority to direct the Commission to develop policies for EU action. Between the 'summit' meetings of national prime ministers, the President of the European Council, the Belgian Herman Van Rompuy, represents the Council within the EU system.

By contrast with the high politics concerns of the European Council, the *Council of Ministers*[3] shares with the European Parliament the power of co-decision on ordinary legislative proposals. The Council and the Parliament act on proposals prepared by the European Commission. National governments are represented in the Council by the Cabinet minister whose department is domestically responsible for issues on the agenda, for example, transport, agriculture, employment, or consumer protection.

Between Council meetings Commission proposals are monitored by national civil servants in the 27 Offices of the Permanent Representatives (PERMREPs) that represent each national government in Brussels. Collectively, they form the Committee of Permanent Representatives (COREPER). It meets weekly to review and sort measures into two categories, those that are 'political', that is, raise issues significant to their national governments, and what the Italians call *leggine*, little laws that are usually narrow in application and technical in content. Such measures are settled by discussions between representatives of national civil servants and the Commission without discussion in the Council of Ministers. The great majority of measures adopted by the EU are little laws.

European institutions have always had a parliamentary assembly, but initially its members were not elected by Europe's citizens. Instead, they were appointed by national parliaments to a part-time 'non-job' without any significant political powers. After almost a quarter-century of lobbying, the popular election of the *European Parliament* (EP) was introduced in 1979 and it has gradually accumulated significant influence. It can question or criticize the actions of individual commissioners and in extreme circumstances vote no confidence in the Commission as a whole. The EP must approve or reject policy proposals by the Commission before they can become law. However, it cannot initiate legislation. This constraint is not imposed by an undemocratic king or Kaiser but by treaties written on behalf of the nationally elected governments of member states.

Members of the European Parliament (MEPs) stand as candidates of national parties in 27 national constituencies. Unlike the Council, which represents national governments, MEPs are organized into multi-national Party Groups that represent partisan differences common across national boundaries, such as socialist, liberal, and green ideologies. The votes of MEPs reflect the policy line laid down by the whips of their multi-national Party Groups (see Chapter 7). If they choose to stand for re-election, and half of MEPs do not, then once in five years they are accountable to their particular national electorate.

A striking innovation of the European Union is that it has institutions that represent supra-national values, goals, and interests. This makes it much more than the sum of the views of national governments. The Treaty of the European Union emphasizes in Article 17 that the *European Commission* represents 'the general interest of the Union'. It does this by promoting EU actions to deal with problems facing member states. As the current Commission President, José Manuel Barroso, puts it, 'The Commission has a unique and historic mission to be more than just a civil service. It is there to speak up for European ideals and values, to take action to support those values, and to defend the European interest.'[4] It has the monopoly power to prepare the initial text of proposed laws and to exercise powers delegated to it by legislation. The 'hotter' the issue and the more interest the Council and Parliament have in setting the agenda, the more the Commission must react to their demands. On less politically contentious issues, the Commission has more scope for influence.

The Commission is divided into Directorates-General (DGs), the equivalent of the ministries of national governments. The priority that the EU has always given to economic integration is reflected in the lopsided distribution of its Directorates. By contrast with the Cabinets of national governments, the Commission has few Directorates dealing with welfare state issues. It also has more Directorates dealing with economic issues. Each Directorate is headed by a Commissioner nominated by a national government. Inasmuch as Commissioners are usually national politicians rather than cosmopolitan diplomats, their national origins provide a starting point for their evaluation of issues, especially if they hope to return to a national political career. However, because Commissioners operate in a multi-national institution with multi-national staff, to be successful their proposals must be endorsed by a big majority of member states and multi-national Groups of MEPs.

Each Directorate is staffed by civil servants recruited on merit from across the continent. Members of the Commission staff are committed to their supra-national employer, and the Commission is responsible for advances towards an ever closer Union. By analogy with bureaucrats, Commission officials are often miscalled Eurocrats. In fact, they are not bureaucrats passively administering laws and policies. Instead, their job is to monitor policies and prepare new measures promoting the interests of their particular Directorate. Professional education and experience within a DG give staff knowledge of specialized fields of EU interest. The most active Commission staff members are policy entrepreneurs; they make use of the Commission's monopoly of proposing policies to advance the interests of their Directorate and of European integration more generally.

By contrast with the Anglo-American emphasis on institutions representing individuals, European states have historically had corporatist institutions representing organized social and economic interests. The EU's *European Economic and Social Committee* (EESC) represents three constituencies: business and financial organizations; trade unions; and a hotch potch third sector for agriculture, professions and not-for-profit welfare organizations. Business members do not speak for citizens but for legal personalities, such as firms and associations of firms. Trade union representatives cannot speak for labour as a whole, because more than two-thirds of the European labour force are not union members. The civil society interests represented in the EESC's third sector share no common characteristic. The EESC's chief function is to represent the views of its constituencies on what they see as the desirability, feasibility and consequences of the Commission's proposals. While lacking the hard power of veto, if the Commission ignores its views, then EESC members have the soft power of representing their objections to national governments and to European Parliament committees that do have hard power.

The enforcement of laws is a necessary condition of effective government; international organizations that cannot do so have more good intentions than judicial teeth. The *European Court of Justice* (ECJ) represents a principle—the rule of law—that holds that governors, whether elected or autocratic, should be held accountable to abstract rules. The judges' constituency is an epistemic community, that is, a group of jurists and lawyers who share common legal values and knowledge. Its 27 judges are each nominated by a national government, but they are expected to be lawyers whose independence is beyond doubt. Before confirmation, they are scrutinized by a panel of European legal experts to ensure that they share common legal norms regardless of their nationality. The Court's chief functions are to adjudicate disputes arising from conflicts between EU and national laws and from uncertainties about EU laws. Unlike American courts, the ECJ prefers to offer legalistic rather than political justifications for its decisions. Nonetheless, by maintaining the supremacy of EU law over national laws, it is a significant political force advancing an ever closer Union.

The introduction of the euro was intended to serve the interest of European integration by replacing national currencies with a European currency and giving the EU a visible attribute of a state. The *European Central Bank* is charged with promoting price stability and economic growth by controlling interest rates and the supply of money in Eurozone states. In an attempt to insulate the Bank from accountability to the major EU institutions in Brussels, its headquarters was placed in Frankfurt am Main, Germany. The immediate constituency of the ECB consists of national central bank officials and professional monetary economists, none of whom is elected. When the euro was launched in 2002, there was confidence in the expertise of monetary economists to prevent inflation and promote long-term economic growth. However, since then the Eurozone crisis has challenged the Bank's expertise and made it more dependent on member states.

The short answer to the question—How do the institutions of the European Union represent European citizens?—is: most don't. EU institutions represent a diversity of interests, principles and other institutions as well as member states and citizens. The European Commission represents the principle of European integration; the Court of Justice the rule of law; and the European Central Bank principles of monetary economics. Members of the Economic and Social Committee represent organized interests of business, labour and professional associations, and NGOs. Although the governments that meet in the European Council are nationally elected, their collective function is, in the words of the Lisbon Treaty, to provide the 'necessary impetus for the development of the Union'. The European Parliament is unique in the EU system in having its members directly elected.

Pluralism is a common feature of the institutions of the European Union. There is an insistence that a plurality of interests as well as countries should be represented in the policymaking process and multiple institutions provide many points of access for representatives of diverse views to raise issues. The upshot is that the short answer to the rhetorical question of Henry Kissinger— Who do I telephone when I want to talk to Europe?—is: one phone call won't do. The European Union is a body with many hands but no head. To arrive at an agreement within the EU is like shaking hands with an octopus.

II Horizontal Accountability Without Vertical Trust

Horizontal accountability involves sharing powers among political institutions; it thus provides a check on absolutist rule, whether by a monarch or a dictator. However, it does not require that the institutions imposing checks be democratically representative. For example, more than two centuries before democratic elections were introduced in England, the Parliament imposed the ultimate check on a monarch; it ordered the beheading of King Charles I. Checks can also give power to undemocratic institutions. For example, the 1982 Turkish Constitution gave the military the right to impose checks on a popularly elected government.

The EU's checks-and-balances system creates lots of horizontal accountability. Before a policy can be adopted, the European Commission is required to discuss its proposals with representatives of national governments in the Committee of Permanent Representatives and the Council of Ministers or European Council; with the European Parliament, representing partisan views; and with the Economic and Social Committee, representing organized interests. The Council and the Parliament have the hard power to withhold approval if they are not satisfied with what the Commission proposes. Once a policy is approved, it may then be checked by the European Court of Justice.

Commission staff now complain of an 'accountability overload', because they are 'having to spend as much time reporting and justifying what they and their colleagues have been doing as they can devote to actually doing things'.[5]

The increase in the EU's collective powers has 'thickened' horizontal accountability by increasing the volume of measures that are subject to scrutiny. The increased powers of the European Parliament have given its many committees the right to act as a check on the Commission. The increased overlap between EU measures and national laws has led officials in national ministries and interest groups to spend more time scrutinizing the details of Commission proposals. Once laws are adopted, comitology procedures enable representations to be made about how they are implemented through discussions in committees of national officials and experts. The emphasis in such discussions tends to be about the technical details of how a policy should work.

The expansion of EU policy has been accompanied by new modes of governance that link EU institutions with those outside the EU system. They include private sector institutions with specialist expertise and non-governmental organizations. In economic and social policy, where the authority of the EU is weak, it promotes what it calls the open method of co-ordination. This encourages representatives of relevant national ministries to meet for discussions of common problems and, if they so choose, to adopt common goals and even policies that converge on the practices of leading member states.

The world financial crisis illustrates the very large number of checks on EU action. National governments under pressure from abroad or at home have been required to reach decisions in a few days. By contrast, many months of discussions among varied EU institutions are normally required to move from non-decisions to decisions on key matters affecting the Eurozone. The German government, which is expected to pledge the most money to deal with an emergency, is now subject to domestic political constraints from its Parliament and from justices of the German high court in Karlsruhe, who see their role as enforcing the German Constitution's requirements for democratic accountability against incursions from Brussels as well as Berlin.

Vertical as well as horizontal checks on governors are required in order to achieve democratic accountability. However, the vertical accountability of Brussels institutions to EU citizens is limited institutionally. The only sanction that European citizens have is very weak, the right to change their vote from one European Parliament election to another. However, this is not the same as the power to turn the government of the day out of office, a defining power in all theories of democracy. Whatever the outcome of an EP election, there is no change in the European Council, the institution giving direction to the EU's political agenda. The membership of the European Commission, the nearest approximation to the executive branch of government, does change after an EP election, but its members are nominated by national governments.

National governments also agree who is President of the Commission and who is President of the European Council.

To hold the EU to account, citizens must have information about policies being formulated or subject to scrutiny within the EU system. The nominal transparency of the EU policy process is lost in the torrent of information that is the daily output of EU institutions. The media that citizens rely on to act as intermediaries between themselves and their government only intermittently report policies being debated in Brussels. A big crisis or a big case of fraud is often required for the media to alert Europe's citizens to what is happening there. Quality media may have a correspondent in Brussels but neither the writers nor the readers of publications such as *The Economist* and the *Financial Times* are representative of European citizens at large. The lack of information about what is happening in Brussels has little effect on accountability, for even if Europe's political citizens were well informed about what the EU is doing, they lack the hard power to hold governors to account.

Decisionmakers in EU institutions do not represent an electoral majority. Instead, they are trustees with substantial discretion to act on behalf of whatever interests or principles they nominally represent. Whether they are trusted by the European citizens that they nominally represent is an empirical question. When the European Commission's Eurobarometer survey asks people about trust in different EU institutions, the replies are similar. Whether the EU institution represents principles, organizations, or people, citizens tend to distrust them (Table 1.1). Even though Members of the European Parliament and the European Council are elected, the European Council is trusted by less than one-third of Europeans and the Parliament by only two-fifths. The economists and policy entrepreneurs of the European Central Bank and the Commission do not rely on votes for trustworthiness, but on doing what they think is best for Europe. However, Europeans are inclined to distrust these institutions too.

Table 1.1. Trust and distrust in EU institutions

Q. Do you tend to trust or not to trust each of these institutions?

	Trust	Distrust (per cent)	Don't know
EU as a whole	34	55	11
European Parliament	41	45	14
European Commission	36	43	21
European Central Bank	36	46	18
European Council	32	41	27

Source: Eurobarometer Survey 76, autumn 2011, questions A10 and A11. Number of respondents: 26,594.

Overall, 55 per cent of Europeans distrust the European Union as a whole. While some European institutions are today more trusted than the political parties and parliaments of many member states, this overlooks an important fact. Citizens who are dissatisfied with the performance of their national government have the hard power of removing it from office at a national election. However, as citizens of the European Union they lack this critical sanction.

III Decisionmaking by Consensus

Effective representation is about influencing policy as well as presenting the views of whoever or whatever is to be represented. To arrive at an EU decision, the process of representation is turned inside out. Instead of voicing demands on behalf of their own constituency, representatives must bargain with those who represent constituencies in 26 other countries. For the EU's institutions to promote an ever closer Union, it must secure closure to otherwise endless deliberations between mutually accountable institutions. Moreover, whatever is agreed must have more 'bite' than the toothless rhetoric that vaguely proclaims the need to do something about Europe's low economic growth or sets ambitious goals for Europe 2020 without specifying the means.

Even though EU institutions have detailed rules about voting, a big majority of decisions are taken by consensus. This elastic term requires approval by substantially more than a single vote but it falls short of unanimity. The appearance of consensus is enhanced by the EU practice of not recording the number of votes against a proposal when a voice vote is taken. A consensus expressed without a recorded vote can variously reflect actual unanimity, 'virtual' unanimity with only one or two objectors, or the support of a substantial majority and the sullen silence of those who do not want to break the consensus norm by voicing their objections. If there appears to be general agreement, the chair of an EU meeting can announce that there is a consensus and put the onus on a dissatisfied participant to challenge this view. A consensus policy may be a compromise that fudges major differences between countries, and therefore risks coming unstuck when political controversy heats up. Nonetheless, by sidestepping a vote EU policymakers can take a step forward toward an ever closer Union.

EU institutions have rules, such as the requirement of a super-majority, that encourage consensus decisionmaking. The Court of Justice of the European Union carries consensus to the extreme. By definition the cases coming before the ECJ involve disagreements about the interpretation of EU law. Nonetheless, the Court seeks to maintain a position above controversy by issuing decisions approved by a majority without recording any dissenting judgment.

The Lisbon Treaty states that decisions of the European Council should be taken by consensus unless otherwise specified, for example, the requirement of unanimity for the endorsement of a treaty. In the Council of Ministers, rules require approval by a Qualified (that is, super) Majority Vote. First of all, a measure needs the endorsement of 73.9 per cent of the votes cast by member states. In addition, a Council proposal must be endorsed by at least two-thirds of member states and a Commission proposal by a majority of states. Thirdly, the states endorsing a measure must constitute at least 62 per cent of the EU's total population. As of November 2014 the barrier to approval will be lowered to require endorsement by the votes of 55 per cent of member states representing at least 65 per cent of the EU's population. On the one hand, these rules favour big states if governments as disparate as those of Britain, Italy, Poland, and Spain agree. On the other hand, the rules also require endorsement by a significant proportion of smaller states, and these countries are more willing to join a consensus than are big states that object to a proposal.

Of the hundreds of measures that come before the Council each year, an overwhelming majority are approved by a consensus without dissent. In the pre-enlargement period 2000–4, an average of 85 per cent were so confirmed and only 15 per cent subject to Qualified Majority Voting. Subsequent to enlargement, more than four-fifths of measures have been approved unanimously. When recorded votes are called, it is often at the behest of one or a few countries that want to cast a symbolic negative vote or make a statement that plays to their domestic political audience but does not create an obstacle to Council approval.

When a national government threatens to invoke the rules to veto a policy requiring unanimity, it loses goodwill and influence over related measures that do not require unanimity. For example, when the European Council met in December 2011 to agree policies about the Eurozone financial crisis, Britain was semi-detached, since it is outside the Eurozone but the City of London is potentially subject to new EU banking regulations. Instead of advancing consensus proposals, Prime Minister David Cameron threatened to veto treaty changes on the euro crisis. The result was a consensus among two dozen member states to exclude Britain from participating in drafting new European financial regulations. In the brutal words of a continental participant, 'Those who do not want to sit around the table with us risk being put on the menu of what will be eaten.'

The European Parliament requires an absolute majority of MEPs to vote approval of a measure. Since the Parliament is fragmented into eight multinational Groups, none of which can come close to commanding an absolute majority, approval requires coalition-building across party lines. Since the whips of Party Groups maintain discipline among their MEPs, an absolute majority can be created by bargaining among Group leaders. Obstacles to a consensus can be finessed by adopting proposals by a voice vote that avoids requiring an MEP to go on record as endorsing a policy contrary to his or her national programme. A big majority of European Parliament measures are endorsed by a voice vote.

The very high volume of measures that come from the Commission each year and the diverse groups that can call the Commission to account places a high premium on participants being willing to compromise. Few issues coming before the Council involve zero-sum outcomes, in which what some countries gain other countries must lose. Most consist of a mixture of elements that can be amended without rejection of a measure's overall intent. Details can be made more widely acceptable by adding a clause, a sentence or a phrase, or removing a line or a few lines to which objection is taken. To achieve consensus, specific interests can be framed in broad and agreeable terms. When participants differ in priorities, they may engage in logrolling, trading support with others in return for endorsement of their priority. The greater the difficulty in arriving at agreement, the more likely it is that no action will be taken or a policy will express the lowest common denominator of agreement, shorn of controversial elements important for making it effective.

The extent to which policymakers are satisfied with the outcome of their negotiations has been evaluated through interviews with PERMREP officials.[6] Satisfaction is measured as the extent to which a Council decision reflects a country's initial position in the process that led up to it. On average, EU decisions result in most countries being more or less satisfied with the relation between their initial aim and the Council's consensus decision. Consistent with the EU's culture of accommodation and compromise, no country is totally satisfied or completely dissatisfied. This suggests that governments are realistic about what they can achieve and tend to pre-adjust their positions in order to have preferences close to what will attract allies in the bargaining process that leads to a consensus. Bigger countries were often less satisfied than small countries; this implies that they have more ambitious goals that cannot be achieved because super-majority rules make it impossible for big countries to impose their views without allies among smaller countries.

The pursuit of consensus is time-consuming; arriving at agreement in a system that has so many checks usually takes years to negotiate and action will come to a halt if no consensus emerges. For these reasons, Romano Prodi, speaking as President of the Commission, argued that the endless search for consensus 'even when there is none to be found' was counterproductive for advancing European integration, because 'progress grinds to a halt'. Instead, Prodi recommended reducing the checks institutionalized in the EU system by adopting 'the normal procedure in a democratic system, a majority voting culture in which decisions reflect the will of the largest number but apply equally to each and every one'.[7]

IV Explanation Is not Justification

Explanation is not the same as justification; it offers an account of why things are as they are. This can be accepted as a justification only on the naive argument of *Candide* that whatever is, is for the best in the best of all possible worlds. Justification gives explicitly normative reasons about how a political system ought to work. If explanation and justification match, this legitimates what the EU is doing. However, the Eurozone crisis is an example of a mismatch. Explaining it as a consequence of past mistakes provides only a 'lesser evil' justification for giving the EU more power over national economies in future. Progress towards an ever closer Union requires popular commitment to ensure the voluntary compliance of governments and citizens with whatever measures are decided in Brussels. When decisions have a visible impact and impose real costs, commitment will be forthcoming only if citizens accept that what the EU is doing is justified.

The multi-level structure of European governance makes national governments the primary institution responsible for justifying what the EU does. A national government that has agreed a measure in Brussels must justify having done so in the course of applying EU decisions as national laws. Once this is done, then citizens are expected to give voluntary compliance because a measure is no longer an EU but a national policy, for which national obligations can be invoked. In this way, for example, governments justify levying Value Added Taxes, which are required by EU law and a portion of which is transferred to Brussels to fund EU policies. Elections provide the justification for citizens accepting measures adopted by their national government. Those who vote for the losing party as well as the governing party are expected to give their consent to whatever their government decides, whether its decisions are taken in the national parliament or in the European Council. If the consequences of an EU measure are nationally unpopular, then citizens have the democratic power to hold their representatives accountable by voting them out of office.

The European Union cannot justify its decisions on the same grounds as a democratically elected national government, because there is no straight line of accountability between voters and the government of the European Union. For example, the European Parliament can vote on legislation but it cannot initiate legislation; this power is in the hands of the European Commission. Moreover, the multi-national Party Groups that combine to determine the legislative output of the Parliament are not directly accountable to voters in the national constituency of any member state. The introduction of direct elections and the expansion of the EP's powers can be compared to early stages of democratization in nineteenth-century Europe. Proposals to end the EU's democratic deficit by turning it into a twentieth-century parliamentary democracy are recurrently made, and recurrently fall flat. Through control of the Council, national governments of contemporary Europe have been successful in preventing the completion of the democratization of the European Union system. The European Parliament does not have the power to elect or eject the members of the Council with which it shares co-decision powers.

Three types of justification are commonly advanced for the powers of the European Union today: history, political values, and effective performance. History is the strongest argument, insofar as it postulates that there is no alternative to accepting the EU as a fact of political life. A variety of political values offer explicit normative justifications for the EU. To justify the EU in terms of its effectiveness is a double-edged sword; doing so implies that if it is ineffective then something should be done to reverse the trend towards an ever closer Union. However, the requirement for super-majorities, concurring majorities, consensus or unanimity makes it difficult to repeal a measure already adopted. When dissatisfaction with the EU arises, the tendency is to rely on the Community method to bring about improvement. Those who argue, like the British eurosceptics, that the EU should return a significant number of its policy responsibilities to member states are marginalized or ignored.

History as explanation. In old democracies such as the United States or Britain, the system of government can be justified by tradition as 'the only one we know'. Tradition hardly fits the European Union. Although the EU is now more than half a century old, the median member state joined as recently as 1995. Thus, hundreds of millions of Europeans have been politically socialized for half their life or longer in a regime that had not yet become part of the EU. Only in the six EU founder states have the great majority of citizens been socialized from childhood to see the EU as part of their multi-level system of government.

Decisions taken in the past are important in giving the European Union a legal rather than an electoral justification through the accumulation of intergovernmental treaties dating back to 1951. Whereas national governments' policies can be altered by the verdict of an electorate, the contents of an international treaty remain unaltered by national election outcomes. In signing an EU treaty a country's government not only commits itself but also binds its successors far into the future. The national leaders sitting in the European Council today have not chosen the terms on which they meet; they have inherited them from predecessors long gone from office and often of a different political persuasion too.

The result of history is the body of EU law known as the *acquis communautaire*. This French term is officially defined as all the EU's treaties, laws, declarations, resolutions, judicial decisions and international agreements of the

Union. It is protected from repeal by an EU norm that once a policy is adopted by a lengthy process of discussion and negotiation, it cannot be opened up for renegotiation at the behest of a member state. This rule confronts applicants for EU membership with a 'take it or leave it' choice; they cannot alter what has been decided before they become a member state. Once a country is an EU member, its national government has the right to question or amend proposals to add more measures to the *acquis*. Each policy that the government of the day endorses then becomes part of the legacy that its successors are bound to accept, even if they would not have given their approval had they represented their country in the Council at the time the measure was adopted.

Theories of path dependence explain the extent to which decisions taken in the distant past still have influence today. Initial decisions not only set the direction in which an organization develops but also impose constraints on subsequent developments. Once these decisions are made, it is politically very difficult to change existing institutions because of the vested interests of those who control and administer them. For example, a large portion of the EU's twenty-first century budget is paid to support agriculture, the chief economic activity of Europe before industrialization began more than a century ago. Even though the problems facing the EU today are very different from those of the immediate post-1945 years, it is politically inefficient to attempt institutional reforms that are costly in time, money and political capital. Over time, changes in the political environment and the shock of events undermine historical justifications and create an opening for fresh policies that need fresh justification.

Justification by political values. To dismiss values as meaningless symbols is to underestimate the role that symbols can play in justifying political action. European values have historically justified conflict rather than consensus. Since the Reformation, Europeans have been divided by religious values. Nationalism, the dominant value of nineteenth-century Europe, was divisive of multi-national empires. Belief in one's national values as being superior to others justified imperialism on other continents and discrimination and worse within Europe. For the first half of the twentieth century many European societies were divided by competing ideologies of liberalism, socialism, and fascism. The European Union has put an end to value conflicts that produced two world wars, but it has not homogenized the values of Europeans.

The preamble to the Lisbon Treaty does enumerate more than a dozen different values as justifying the European Union. The problem is: which values are most important? Furthermore, many of the values invoked—freedom, liberty, and the rule of law—are found on all continents; they are not restricted to Europe. The American Constitution endorsed these values more than a century before they were commonly endorsed by European states. Norway and Switzerland show that EU membership is not necessary for a European country to endorse the values that the European Union claims to represent. The most distinctive value in the EU treaties is the commitment to an ever closer Union.

The European Union would not have come into existence if national policy-makers had regarded national identity as an overriding and exclusive value. Nor could it have succeeded if the existence of a European identity was a necessary condition of developing political institutions with powers to make decisions binding on the diverse peoples and nations of Europe. Social science surveys find that about half of Europeans, when asked, are prepared to identify themselves as Europeans as well as identifying with their own nation. However, this identity is secondary not primary. Major European events followed by hundreds of millions of Europeans, such as the Eurovision song contest and European Cup football matches, remain competitions between national champions.

The European Union was initially justified as the best means of preventing Germany and France going to war for the fourth time since 1870 and also of creating a modern, prosperous economy. The successes of the EU have made inconceivable another war and a return to national economies closed to trade with other countries. For believers in European integration as a value in itself, the achievement of historic objectives does not make the EU obsolete. Instead, it justifies whatever new measures are expected to advance integration, whether they are small, such as the requirement of metric labels on drinks sold for consumption in non-metric Britain, or big, such as turning the Euro-zone into a fiscal as well as a monetary Union.

Justification by effectiveness. Functionalists argue that the best justification of the EU is the effectiveness of its policy outputs rather than the representative-ness of the institutions that make its decisions. The EU is seen as a government of trustees acting for the people rather than being a government of or by the people. From this perspective, complaints that EU institutions lack account-ability to European citizens are irrelevant and attempts to reform EU insti-tutions to remove the democratic deficit are unnecessary. The effectiveness of a policy is sufficient to justify the institutions that made it.

The European Union's claim to act is clearest in policy areas requiring collective action that national governments cannot take on their own. The single European market, for example, requires collective action to remove barriers to the free movement of thousands of goods and services between dozens of countries across a continent. When national governments face problems too big to be resolved on their own, their leaders can invoke national interest to justify turning to Brussels to take decisions. The 'reach' of public policies across national borders varies enormously. Preventing environmental pollution is an 'intermestic' issue involving domestic and international agree-ments because it requires controlling rivers such as the Rhine that wend through many member states. By contrast, laws regulating marriage and divorce are taken nationally and the provision of public libraries and swimming pools are local matters.

Giving priority to effectiveness assumes that there is a consensus about both means and ends. For example, the introduction of the Eurozone was supported by economists believing it would be effective in producing economic benefits and by policymakers favouring it as a big step towards an ever closer Union. The two justifications were often combined in a single speech or pamphlet. However, many political issues raise differences of opinion about both. Justification by effectiveness becomes politically controversial when it distributes costs and benefits visibly and unequally between member states or groups of EU citizens. For example, rising unemployment has made the EU's policy of the free movement of workers across the EU controversial in West European countries where the positive effects on a country's Gross Domestic Product of immigrants from Eastern Europe are less visible than perceived threats to existing jobs.

Giving priority to effectiveness encourages technocracy, and EU institutions make much use of experts with specialist knowledge in such fields as air-traffic safety or the capital requirements of banks. Within communities of experts, there is a common trans-national method for analysing problems facing the EU and shared knowledge often leads to a consensus about what policy the EU should adopt. The credential for belonging to a community of experts is a PhD or a professorship rather than success in winning elections. The recommendations of technocrats are justified by who they are rather than by whom they represent.

The crisis of the Eurozone is an extreme example of the risk of justifying European integration by effectiveness. National governments placed their national currency in the hands of technocrats in the European Central Bank in a Faustian bargain in which they expected to receive benefits without costs. For a time, their expectations were met. However, as in Faust's pact with the Devil, the Eurozone crisis has shown that no policy is permanently effective. Countries that have been enjoying its benefits must now pay their debts and national governments in the Eurozone must find fresh ways of justifying paying the costs of a central EU policy that now delivers visible costs.

2

Forging an Ever Closer Union

We can proceed with a zig here and a zag there.

Jean Monnet

The uniting of Europe is a very old idea. Two millennia ago half the continent was unified by the armies and administrators of the Roman Empire. Adolf Hitler's brief control of the whole of the continent prompted its victims to create a Union based on common interests rather than conquest. In rejecting the past, the founders drew on personal experience. The Father of Europe, the French Foreign Minister Robert Schuman, was by birth both German and Luxembourgeois; he became a French citizen as a consequence of France being on the winning side in the First World War. Konrad Adenauer became Chancellor of the fourth German regime in which he had lived. The Italian prime minister, Alcide de Gasperi, had lived in five regimes, one Austrian, one Papal, and three Italian. The European Union's founders succeeded where Napoleon, Lenin, and Hitler failed. It now has far more powers and capacity for action than its near contemporary, the United Nations.

To meet the multiple problems of reconstructing Europe, the initial plan was to create a European Defence Community, an Economic Community, and a Political Community. The idea was that both the Defence and Economic Communities would be supervised by a Political Community with a supra-national Executive accountable to a bicameral parliament with a popularly elected chamber and a chamber representing national parliaments. The French Assembly's rejection of the proposed Defence Community in 1954 buried plans for a Political Community. This left the Economic Community as the only institution taking the first step towards an ever closer Union.

The Treaty of Rome that created the European Economic Community (EEC) in 1957 conferred few powers on the new institution, but its ambition was great. The preamble of the Treaty declared that the EEC was 'laying the foundations of an ever closer Union among the peoples of Europe'. Member states accepted its supra-national authority for different reasons. Germany saw it as a step forward from military defeat and control by occupying powers. For France it was a means of protecting and expanding its political influence. In the words of Charles de Gaulle, the point of Europe was 'to prevent domination either by the Americans or the Russians'.[1] For the Benelux countries of Belgium, the Netherlands, and Luxembourg it was a means of gaining recognition as partners with big states when decisions were taken.

Britain refused to join. As Jean Monnet saw it, 'Britain has not been conquered or invaded. She felt no need to exorcise history'.[2] Instead, most of its leaders accepted Winston Churchill's definition of Britain as having three roles: at the centre of a global empire, a special relationship with the United States, and sufficient influence in Europe to prevent any one country from dominating it. Hugh Gaitskell, the leader of the Labour Party when Harold Macmillan sought to join Europe in the early 1960s, opposed doing so on the grounds that it would get rid of a thousand years of history—failing to note that the start of the millennium was marked by the success in 1066 of Norman French conquerors reclaiming England for Europe.

The early treaties of the European Union concentrated on replacing the protectionist economic policies of European states with policies promoting a common market. The idea was hardly new; Britain had adopted free trade in 1846 and the American economy owed its success to the United States being a common market. It was nonetheless novel when compared with the German tradition of *Nationalwirtschaft* (national economy) or the French practice of mercantilism. By concentrating on a common market, the promoters of European integration sought to avoid taking sides between socialist, Catholic, and liberal parties with differing ideas about what principles should govern a market.

A zig-zag strategy of taking whatever steps were possible to achieve a closer *Union* has led to the deepening and broadening of the EU's powers. These shorthand terms refer to two complementary methods for advancing European integration. Deepening increases the impact of policies in fields in which the EU has long been active. It has resulted in tens of thousands of pages of laws and regulations that now affect everything from goods sold across national borders to the measure of a beer in an English pub. Broadening refers to the extension of the scope of EU policymaking far beyond a narrow concern with tariffs and agricultural products. For example, the Erasmus programme adopted in 1987 has resulted in more than three million Europeans studying outside their home country for a semester or more. Today the European Union not only promotes a single European market but also has powers concerning justice, home affairs, and security.

Each EU measure has been locked in place by the doctrine of the *acquis communautaire*, which holds that the repeal of any collective commitment

embodied in an EU treaty requires unanimous consent. The political significance of this term can colloquially be translated as: there is no going back from
the path we are on.

I The Forward March of Treaties

Treaties are more than the foundation stones of the EU; they are also its
building blocks, because each new treaty confers new powers on EU institutions. The authority of treaties gives EU institutions the legal powers to turn
policy aspirations into laws. Collectively, the treaties of the EU are the equivalent of a national constitution. The Lisbon Treaty, which came into force in
2009, consolidates an accumulation of half a century of treaties in two parts; a
Treaty on European Union and the Treaty on the Functioning of the European
Union. Treaties confer powers on EU institutions; set out procedures for
making policies; and formally incorporate practices that have grown up infor-
mally. Since each treaty is lengthy, its adoption has much more impact on the
activities of the EU than the typical amendment of a national constitution.
Moreover, while the term of office of the national governments approving a
treaty is limited, the treaties that they approve endure. Treaties entrench the
EU's powers in a form that protects them from future challenge or reversal.

Constructing a constitution piecemeal. In one critical respect, the EU's building
of a constitution differs from normal practice: it does not involve citizens
directly. No EU treaty has ever been endorsed by referendums held in a majority
of member states (see Figure 5.1). Moreover, the treaties are not prepared by a
popularly elected constitutional convention. Instead, the normal practice of
international law is followed; a national government is assumed to represent
the position of all its citizens. An EU treaty is prepared in an Intergovernmental
Conference of the governments of member states; most of the drafting
is done by committees of EU officials and representatives of national governments. A draft treaty is then subject to intergovernmental bargaining
before it can secure the unanimous approval of governments. In addition,
it requires endorsement by the national parliaments of all member states. It
is sufficient for it to be signed by 27 heads of state. Since 1986 an EU treaty
has been signed at the rate of one every four years. The most recent treaty,
the Lisbon Treaty, came into effect in 2009.

The first treaty was modest in scope. The 1951 European Coal and Steel
Community (ECSC) concerned two industries in parts of Europe with histor-
ically indeterminate boundaries. Alsace and Lorraine had been intermittently
German and French during the previous century. In 1945 France occupied the
German Saar but France had no claim to the coal and steel of the Ruhr region.
Additional coal resources in Belgium and Luxembourg, both relatively new

states with porous boundaries, justified their inclusion. Monnet's vision of the ECSC as the political foundation for European integration meant that the Netherlands and Italy were also included as founder states.

In retrospect the ECSC was important because it created a supra-national executive composed of technocratic experts acting as 'the repository of the European General Will, as against evil governments merely the spokesmen for particular selfish political wills' and a court to enforce decisions.[3] It did not claim to be popularly representative nor did it require the creation of a common identity between peoples who had been at war six years previously. The six founder members formed an intergovernmental Council with the power to approve or amend the executive's plans. Monnet's design thus rejected the idea that the Community should simply be a meeting place in which industrial enterprises and affected unions would engage in horse-trading about their respective interests. While the economic significance of coal and steel has waned, European institutions have grown by building on the ECSC's foundations.

The European Economic Community gave wider scope to the potential for advancing political unity by promoting economic integration. Unlike the ECSC, it had the power to remove tariffs and quotas on most forms of trade among member states and to set tariffs on imports from non-member states. Political realism meant that market principles did not apply uniformly. The Common Agricultural Policy, a protectionist measure described as a welfare state for peasants, was of major importance in securing approval by France and Italy for pro-market measures benefiting German industry.

The economic boom that made the 1960s a decade of affluence benefited both national governments and the EU. National governments took credit for borders secure against threats from neighbours, the consolidation of democracy in former dictatorships, and economies generating tax revenues sufficient to finance the development of a generous welfare state. European Union leaders took credit for laying foundations for an unprecedented period of peace and prosperity. The attractions of the EU were sufficient for Britain to join in 1973, along with Ireland and Denmark.

Deepening political integration has required the replacement of decision-making by unanimity with consensus decisionmaking. This began after Charles de Gaulle triggered an empty-chair crisis in 1965 by boycotting meetings of the European Council in order to prevent the implementation of decisions that would have deprived France of its veto on EU measures. The impasse was resolved by an agreement high on elasticity and low on clarity, the Luxembourg Compromise. It stipulated that any decision affecting 'a very important national interest' would be deferred until unanimity could be reached. In 1982 the British government tried to invoke the Compromise against French interests. It claimed that budget proposals for agricultural subsidies violated a vital British interest in cheap food; the claim was rejected. The following year the Council endorsed treaty provisions for a Qualified Majority Vote as part of a solemn declaration to advance towards ever closer Union.

The expansion of EU powers led to national governments accepting the direct election of the European Parliament in place of an appointive assembly (see Chapter 6). A quarter of a century after the ECSC was founded, the Single European Act deepened and broadened the EU's powers for action. The EU gained more scope to act in fields previously reserved for national governments, such as the environment, technology policy, and research. The Act also conferred greater powers to promote social and economic cohesion through policies on employment, working conditions, living conditions, education and vocational training, and the rights of minorities. It broadened the number of policies that could be decided by a Qualified Majority Vote. Margaret Thatcher, a leading proponent of a single European market, was prepared to accept a reduction in the requirement of unanimity in order to prevent protectionist member states from having a veto that could be used to prevent what she saw as the EU's primary goal, the creation of a common market.

A big symbolic step forward was taken when the 1992 Maastricht Treaty renamed the EEC the European Union. In an effort to bring the peoples of Europe closer, European citizenship was conferred on everyone who was already a citizen of a member state. However, instead of turning passive into active support, public opinion surveys showed that it had no impact on those who doubted the desirability of EU expansion.[4] The European Parliament gained the right of co-decision with the Council, requiring each institution to endorse many measures before they could take effect as law. The Treaty extended the Union's economic powers by authorizing an Economic and Monetary Union. It also proclaimed an intention to broaden powers in two traditional defining activities of the state: foreign and security policy, and justice and home affairs.

The new powers of the Maastricht Treaty did not increase public support for European integration. Instead, the Treaty stimulated a minority to express their opposition to further integration, thus undermining the permissive consensus that had previously allowed integration to proceed by elite bargains. In Britain, for example, where many had seen the single European market as a triumph in expanding economic impact of integration while limiting its political impact, there was a reaction against extending the EU's powers. Rebellious Conservative MPs and Labour opponents almost succeeded in voting down the Maastricht Treaty.

As a sop to those who wanted to limit the scope of the Union, the Maastricht Treaty declared that where both the EU and member states have the power to act, the principles of subsidiarity and proportionality should apply.

These principles are defined as justifying EU action only when a policy object-ive can be 'better achieved at the Union level' rather than by member states acting on their own (Article 5). In practice, decisions about where the line ought to be drawn have been taken in Brussels. There the dominant view is that the Community method of decisionmaking is better than leaving matters in the hands of member states.

The increase in the scope of the EU's powers has met with some resistance. To get around this, member states have begun to form coalitions of the willing. The Schengen Treaty, abolishing the need for border checks and passports on movement between member states, has evolved from an agree-ment between a few member states to an agreement that covers more than three-quarters of the EU's 27 member states. The practice of enhanced co-operation was formally recognized in the 1997 Amsterdam Treaty. It allows states that 'constructively abstain' in a Council vote to opt out of policies approved by a big majority of member states. The Lisbon Treaty has gone further in facilitating enhanced co-operation.

In response to mounting criticisms that the EU confined policymaking to a narrow circle in Brussels, the 2001 Laeken Declaration of the European Coun-cil called for the European Union to be 'more democratic, more transparent and more efficient'. The Convention on a Constitution for Europe was estab-lished under the chairmanship of the former French President Valéry Giscard d'Estaing. In the words of the Vice Chair, former Italian premier Giuliano Amato, the aim was to produce a baby not a bun, that is, a Constitution that would mature into a federal state rather than a bun that remained constant in size or went stale.

The forward march of EU treaties without involving Europe's citizens was challenged by the symbolic and practical political importance of approving a Constitution for Europe. A number of governments asked their citizens to endorse it in a referendum. After four referendums were held, the result showed no consensus. A majority in Spain and Luxembourg endorsed the Constitution, but a majority in France and the Netherlands rejected it (see Chapter 4). EU leaders did not interpret rejection as showing that Europe's citizens opposed carrying integration further. Instead, almost all of its sub-stantive content, shorn of the symbols of statehood that embellished the draft Constitution, were repackaged as the Lisbon Treaty. Policy competences in such fields as energy, climate change, and tourism were expanded and the posts of President of the European Council and of EU High Representative for Foreign Affairs and Security were created. The co-decision powers of the European Parliament were enhanced.

To avoid another frustration, governments in France and the Netherlands did not consult their citizens through referendums. The Danish government prevailed on its Ministry of Justice to find legal grounds for avoiding a constitutionally required referendum. In Britain the Conservative opposition called for a referendum, but this call was rejected by the Labour government. Only in Ireland was avoidance of a referendum impossible. When Irish voters rejected the Treaty in a low turnout referendum, a second referendum was called. The Lisbon Treaty was approved and came into effect in December 2009.

Because EU treaties require unanimous approval by all member states, the EU has engaged in legal contortions to avoid having to follow this procedure in assuming new EU powers over national economies, since Britain would then have a veto. Nonetheless, the key document signed by 25 member states is called the Treaty on Stability, Coordination and Governance. However, formal legality is a weak basis for justifying the commitment of Europe's citizens to rules that are intended to limit the power of their national government over national budgets.

Mission creep. Treaties are incomplete contracts; their future development is not fixed. There is lots of space between their black-letter lines to be filled in subsequently by political agreement. A treaty, like a constitution, must be flexible enough to change when the facts change. The United States government acts today in ways unforeseen and unforeseeable by the eighteenth-century authors of its Constitution. The unwritten British Constitution has been adapted to circumstances very different from those that faced medieval monarchs.

In signing a treaty a country's government commits not only itself but also its successors far into the future. However, much that it signs up to is vague. Treaties conferring powers on the European Union are full of expansive declarations but often short on detail. For example, Article 3 of the Lisbon Treaty states the objectives of promoting peace, freedom, security, justice, solidarity, equality, and other goals of groups that influenced its drafting. However, identifying goals is easier than formulating policies to attain them. Because the goals are political, they are subject to dispute. For example, a key advocate of the Single European Act, Margaret Thatcher, saw it as the means of removing barriers to competition in goods and services. However, the Maastricht Treaty subsequently endorsed economic and social cohesion, which socialists such as Jacques Delors have interpreted as a mandate for imposing regulations on Thatcher's free-market vision. In effect, EU treaties create an arena in which the development of the EU is contested.

Jean Monnet saw the founding treaties as starting a dynamic process in which EU policies were gradually advanced through *engrenage*, a French term meaning getting caught up in the gears of machinery. The term has been translated into English as spillovers; in Washington it is described as mission creep. The result is that 'a given action, related to a specific goal, creates a situation in which the original goal can be assured only by taking further actions, which in turn creates a further condition and a need for more'.[5] The spillover theory explains how one damned policy leads to another, since resolving one problem directs attention to new problems and opportunities for EU action. In Aaron Wildavsky's phrase, 'Policy becomes its own cause.'[6] A treaty assigning powers to an EU institution starts a process in which relatively narrow EU measures have consequences that spill over into related areas. For example, measures taken under the Single European Act to promote labour mobility between member states have consequences for claims to social security and the right of EU citizens to vote wherever they live in Europe. Critics call such an expansion of powers empire-building.

Policy entrepreneurs are quick to see interconnections between policies. To a policy entrepreneur, the legal powers conferred on the EU in successive treaties are a hunting licence for expanding activities. Steady pressure toward an ever closer Union is maintained by the multi-national staff of the European Commission. When a problem arises, the response of the Commission staff reflects its commitment to the Community method, the principle that the EU is best able to determine policies to deal with member states. The enactment of Commission proposals depends on support from the European Parliament, which actively supports an ever closer Union, and the Council, whose political members take little interest in the technical measures that constitute the pebble-by-pebble expansion of the beachheads that treaties offer to the Commission.

The iron cage of the acquis. In moving towards an ever closer Union, decisions taken early in the history of an institution tend to persist along the same path. The doctrine of the *acquis communautaire* means that in signing a Treaty a country's government of the day not only commits itself but also commits its successors far into the future. Because the number of laws and regulations contained in the *acquis* grows as decisions are taken each year, it cumulatively ratchets up progress towards an ever closer Union.

A legacy of EU commitments confronts each newly elected national government with a fait accompli. The policies that the European Union carries out today have not been approved by the national governments currently belonging to the European Council or by the current Parliament of MEPs. They are commitments inherited from long-retired or dead politicians. For example, official EU documents today coyly label budget commitments arising from the Common Agricultural Policy as green measures. In fact, much of the money spent is a legacy of a 1950s decision to support France's large and economically inefficient system of peasant agriculture.

For each of the 21 countries that were not founder states of the European Union, the *acquis* means that they must accept all the laws and regulations adopted before they joined the EU. British prime ministers find it particularly difficult to accept this practice, because it is inconsistent with the doctrine that no Parliament can bind its successor. When confronted with the binding reality of EU commitments, Margaret Thatcher reacted with the instinctive cry, 'No, no, no'. However, each British prime minister has had to accept what previous prime ministers have endorsed, even if they were not old enough to vote when this was done—or, if they voted, they had voted against the government that signed a treaty. This explains the animus that leads many Conservatives to demand a national referendum to nullify the application of major EU policies to Britain or even to withdraw completely from the EU.

II The Depth and Breadth of Policies

Whereas treaties and constitutions define what government is, policies define what government does. A public policy requires three resources: laws in order for government to act, money to meet its cost, and employees to deliver the policy. The mixture of resources varies between policies; for example, EU consumer-protection policies are law-intensive while payments to agricultural producers are money-intensive. When policies are labour-intensive, such as inspecting health and safety conditions in factories, delivery is in the hands of employees of member states. The European Union is distinctive in its profile of resources; its lawmaking powers are much greater than its taxing and spending powers and the number of its employees.

Laws are the European Union's greatest resource and EU treaties place no limit on the number that it can adopt. By the time of the negotiations for the 2004 enlargement of the EU, the *acquis* had already grown to 36 subject-matter chapters and more than 80,000 pages of laws. It now bulks larger still. The chief constraint on lawmaking is political: enactment requires acceptance by the multiple institutions involved in the EU's decisionmaking process. In a typical year the Commission will propose more than a thousand laws. Insofar as compliance involves costs, these are met by the national governments administering EU decisions and by organizations subject to their effects.

The measures implementing the EU's powers differ in how they are adopted and how they take effect. Ordinary legislative acts, the equivalent of a national Act of Parliament, are taken by a co-decision process requiring approval by an absolute majority of the European Parliament and a Qualified Majority of the Council of Ministers. More than half of EU measures may be adopted without detailed consideration by the Parliament or the Council; they are scrutinized by Commission and national government officials working through the Committee on Permanent Representatives. Directives are instructions to member states to enact national legislation that will achieve the results set out in a Brussels proposal. Formal decisions are binding on those to whom they are addressed, for example, businesses engaging in cartel-like behaviour that restricts competition. Recommendations and opinions are exhortations without binding legal effect.

The breadth of topics on which the European Union can legislate is narrower than that of member states. The latter have kept in their own hands primary control of such fields as criminal law, family law, education, and health. Three-quarters of EU legislation concerns activities that are related to the stream of commerce in a single European market. They include laws about agriculture and fisheries, industry and competition, the free movement of goods, money and persons, and the environment. One in five laws deals with external and security affairs; however, most of these are relatively narrow measures affecting a particular feature of the EU's relations with a single state. The remainder of EU legislation regulates how its own institutions operate; very little deals with the rights of citizens.

The EU's powers to regulate a market of half a billion people give it international clout. The Commission has been more successful than American anti-trust regulators in using its powers to force leading American firms to stop practices that restrict competition. In a battle between the Commission and Microsoft, the Commission won. Microsoft was not only forced to change its behaviour in order to continue selling its products in Europe, but also paid an 800 million euro fine. Microsoft has put the lesson to good use. It led a group of companies making a complaint to the Commission about Google acting in restraint of trade. After undergoing a lengthy investigation by the Commission, in July 2012 Google agreed to drop practices privileging its own products as against those of competitors in order to avoid a long legal battle and the risk of a billion euro fine.

The EU is not involved in the hands-on administration of its measures; for this it depends on middle- to lower-ranking officials in national, regional, and local authorities. The translation of EU measures into national laws provides some leeway for interpreting the intent of Brussels. The text may be vague, because it fudged disagreements at the European level. The great majority of EU measures are placed on national statute books in a reasonable amount of time. When a member state is slow to implement a law or fails to do so, the Commission can take the matter to the European Court of Justice. When domestic politics gives a strong incentive not to comply, then a national government may prefer a Court case so that, if it does go along with Brussels, it is seen to do so because of a Court order. The ECJ normally finds in favour of the primacy of EU law and can impose fines of millions of euros if a country fails to comply. The leading countries subject to court actions for non-compliance are Italy, Belgium, and Greece.

Given the EU's population and the scope of its powers, it has very few *employees*. The Commission's staff of about 26,000 permanent employees is far less than the million or so public employees in the average EU member state and more than 50 million public employees in the EU as a whole. The EU's multi-national character results in one-tenth of its employees being interpreters at meetings or translating EU documents into its 23 official languages. The annual cost of the EU's 'faceless bureaucracy' is 13 euros per European citizen each year, a pittance compared to the cost of public administration in member states.

The Commission can deal with its many responsibilities with so few employees because it does not directly administer the great majority of the policies that it adopts. Instead, this responsibility is given to employees of the national governments of member states. Sometimes they do so along with administering national laws, for example, monitoring health and safety at work. The EU's lack of hands on control of spending strengthens the continental tendency to impose detailed controls on how money is spent in efforts to reduce favouritism and corruption. Whatever the language of the controls, the result is red tape.

In absolute terms the annual *revenue* of the EU appears vast; it is more than 140bn euros. This is eight times greater than the revenue of the United Nations and greater than the national revenue of 12 EU member states. However, EU revenue is barely one per cent of the collective Gross Domestic Product of member states. It is also small by comparison with what member states collect from their national citizens; the median country's tax revenue is about 40 times the sum it contributes to the EU's coffers.

The EU does not collect tax revenue directly; this remains the responsibility of member states. Instead, it is forwarded a portion of the revenue that member states collect from their citizens. Three-quarters of its revenue is derived from a levy on each state's Gross National Income. Less than one-eighth comes from a share of the Value Added Tax that each national government collects. A similar amount comes from tariffs that the EU levies on imports from outside the EU trade area and a miscellany of agricultural levies. The EU's income is related to each state's total economic activity, a formula that takes into account both a country's ability to pay and its population. Among smaller countries similar in population, those that are prosperous, such as Sweden, contribute up to twice as much money as those that are not, such as Portugal and Hungary. Germany, the state with the most people and the biggest Gross National Income, makes the largest contribution to the EU's revenue, just over one-sixth of its total. Although the populations of France, Italy, and Britain are similar in size, Britain contributes less than the other two because of Margaret Thatcher's success in arguing that Britain deserves a rebate because it receives much less back from the EU in agricultural subsidies.

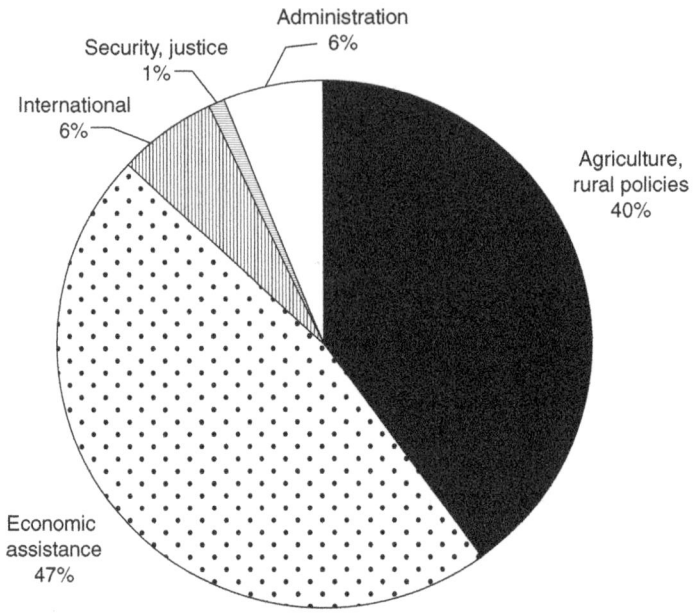

Figure 2.1. How the EU spends its money

Source: Statement of Estimates of the Commission, Brussels, 25.4. 2012, SEC (2012) 270, p. 82.

EU *expenditure* is distinctive in what it supports (Figure 2.1). Spending to promote economic development and assistance to poorer regions claims 47 per cent of the EU budget. These policies are ambitiously described as advancing social cohesion within member states and between the EU's poorer and better off countries. Although farmers constitute little more than one per cent of the EU's population and two per cent of its labour force, agricultural and related programmes claim two-fifths of the EU budget. EU programmes pay farmers for crops they produce and sometimes for crops that they do not produce; for land management practices described as environmentally friendly; and for infrastructure useful in rural areas.

Entitlement to EU funds is driven by complex formulas that allocate funds according to specific economic and social criteria. Agricultural subsidies can be claimed only in rural areas and economic aid requires high unemployment or a low standard of living in some or all regions of a country. The formulas for entitlements are the result of intense political bargaining among founder states, subsequently amended after the enlargement of the European Union. There has been a shift from supporting declining industries such as shipbuilding to encouraging activities intended to promote economic growth. France and Spain receive the largest absolute amount of EU funds, 13 billion euros each, because they are populous and still have relatively large agricultural sectors. Second equal in receiving funds are Poland, which still has a large agricultural population, and Germany, with twice the population of Poland.

The chief spending programmes of the EU produce visible benefits, for example, cash subsidies paid to farmers or research grants paid to multinational networks of universities. The funds for these programmes do not come from taxes that the EU levies on its citizens but from taxes that national governments collect. Likewise, the costs of many EU regulations are not visible to voters; they fall on business enterprises rather than individual citizens.

The EU also engages in off the books taxing and spending. Some EU laws impose compliance costs on national governments responsible for administering them and on business enterprises required to meet EU employment and environmental regulations. The European Central Bank's rules about how national governments should manage their finances were intended to bring major benefits to national economies in the form of lower inflation and greater economic growth. However, the Eurozone crisis has shown that ECB policies can impose costs on both national governments that have been lax in complying, as the Bank expected, and on the countries that are expected to fund measures that deal with the Eurozone crisis.

The absolute size of *EU expenditure* is overshadowed by that of member states. The EU spends only 280 euros for each citizen. By contrast, even though the United Kingdom has less than one-eighth the population of the European Union, its total public expenditure is more than six times that of the EU budget. Absent from the EU's budget is significant expenditure on the big-ticket policies that consume the bulk of public expenditure in member states. The EU does not have a big defence budget because it has no army. Nor does it spend on servicing public debt because it cannot engage in deficit financing as member states do. Whereas member states finance social security programmes by paying pensions to more than 100 million Europeans, the EU pays pensions only to its small number of retired employees. Nor does the EU fund teachers or health-service workers whose salaries make big claims on the budgets of national governments. Two of the three pillars of EU policy—Justice and Home Affairs, and Foreign Affairs and Security—receive very little from the EU budget.

The net national benefit of EU spending reflects its national income, population, and specific economic circumstances (Table 2.1). The larger a country's per capita national income, the more it must pay to the EU. The lower a country's per capita national income, the less it pays and the stronger its claim for funds to finance economic development. Eligibility for agricultural and rural subsidies does not depend on national income or population but on economic geography; hence, French and German farmers as well as East European farmers benefit.

Table 2.1. What countries pay and get from Brussels

	Contributes	Receives	Net balance
	€ mns	€ mns	€ per capita
Luxembourg	261	1,554	2,530
Estonia	142	807	496
Lithuania	269	1,601	411
Greece	2,310	5,748	303
Latvia	175	843	300
Hungary	955	3,650	270
Portugal	1,847	4,378	238
Slovakia	647	1,905	231
Poland	3,656	11,822	214
Czech Republic	1,497	3,415	182
Slovenia	387	756	180
Ireland	1,394	2,065	150
Belgium	4,783	6,145	125
Malta	61	112	122
Bulgaria	352	1,222	116
Spain	10,095	13,190	67
Romania	1,143	2,317	55
Cyprus	184	178	−7
Finland	1,702	1,309	−73
Italy	15,332	9,497	−96
Austria	2,626	1,821	−96
France	19,580	13,105	−99
United Kingdom	14,659	6,745	−127
Germany	23,772	11,825	−146
Denmark	2,380	1,525	−154
Sweden	3,243	1,646	−170
Netherlands	5,613	2,146	−208

Source: European Commission. <http://ec.europa.eu/budget/library/biblio/publications/2010/fin_report/fin_report_10_data_en.pdf.> Data for 2010.

The biggest net recipients of EU funds are Estonia and Lithuania, after discounting the unique position of Luxembourg as a small country with a large number of EU offices. Each receives more than 400 euros per person; Greece and Latvia are also big net beneficiaries of the EU budget. In all, 17 member states are net beneficiaries of EU funding including 11 of the 12 countries admitted in the 2004/7 enlargement round. The countries that make the largest net contribution to the EU budget, Germany and France, are populous and the Netherlands, Sweden, and Denmark are the biggest net contributors per capita.

III Do Europeans Want an Ever Closer Union?

The accumulation of powers by the European Union through big bang treaties and mission creep is a tribute to the skill of the founders in creating dynamic institutions. However, the views of Europe's citizens are problematic, for they have never been directly consulted about the growth of the European Union. Moreover, at a time when decisions in Brussels are becoming more important, more visible, and at times more costly, the passive consent of Europe's citizens can no longer be taken for granted.

The evaluation of popular attitudes toward European integration is confused by the static and dynamic meanings of this term. Satisfaction with European integration as it is today is not proof of a demand for more of the same. Instead, citizens who are satisfied with the status quo can favour no change, on the grounds that it is good enough as it is, and this is even more likely to be true of people with no opinion. Likewise, dissatisfaction is not necessarily a sign of wanting less integration. The strongest partisans of an ever closer Union use dissatisfaction with current conditions to promote further integration. For example, the President of the Commission uses the EU's limited powers to deal with the Eurozone crisis as an argument for moving toward a federation of states. In a complementary manner, people who think that integration has gone too far are not necessarily endorsing withdrawal from the European Union. They may simply want to see specific powers returned from Brussels to their national government. This prospect is particularly likely as and when the new EU powers over national budgets begin to bite. Even if the demand of extremely anti-EU Britons was met for the United Kingdom to withdraw from the European Union, this would not lead to the EU's disintegration. There are provisions in the Lisbon Treaty for an individual country to withdraw. British withdrawal could even be welcomed by proponents of integration as taking the brakes off the development of a European federation.

The European Election Study (EES) provides evidence about whether people think European unification should go further or has already gone too far (Figure 2.2). The question it asks avoids associating the principle of integration with specific policies that could influence replies. For example, linking integration with protection of the environment would make it appear more desirable while linking it with transferring money from more prosperous to less prosperous member states would make it less attractive. A distinctive feature of the EES question is that it effectively offers a Goldilocks option, that is, a third choice, neither more nor less integration on an 11-point scale ranging from 0 to 10. People who do not favour change in either direction can position themselves at the scale's mid-point, 5.

Whereas Brussels is unequivocally committed to an ever closer Union, most Europeans are not. There is a three-way division of public opinion; the largest group is the median group, the 30 per cent in favour of things as they are. There is a mixture of motives for taking this middle-of-the-road position. Some are ambivalent, seeing it as having a mixture of advantages and

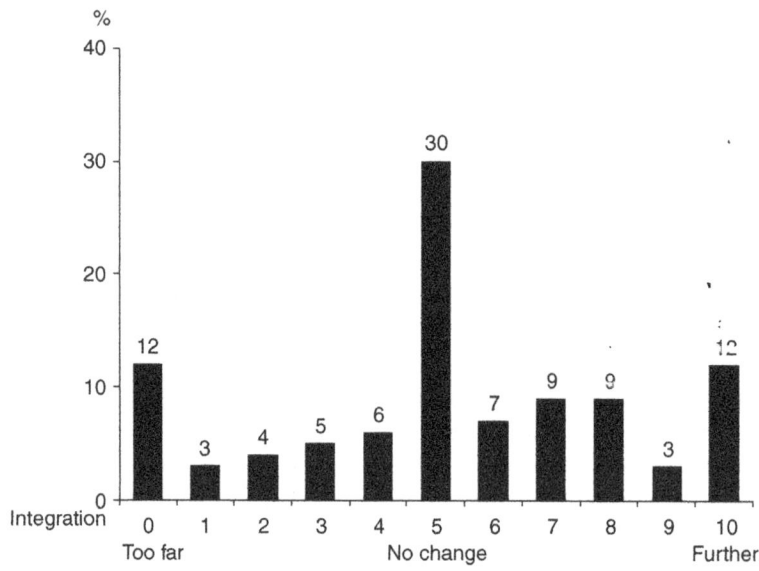

Figure 2.2. Median European favours leaving EU as it is
Source: European Election Survey, 2009. Number of respondents in 27 countries: 27,069.

disadvantages. Others are indifferent; as long as the EU appears irrelevant to their lives they have no opinion. Instead of having ideologically fixed views for or against integration, those in the middle are likely to judge integration pragmatically, being favourable if it is seen as bringing benefits, and opposing more integration if it does not.

Among Europeans who do have an opinion about European integration, four in ten support it going further while three in ten think integration has already gone too far (Figure 2.2). However, the views of Europeans are not polarized. The central tendency in opinion is moderate, endorsing the status quo or favouring just a little more or a little less integration. The extreme ends of the scale are not asked to endorse a United States of Europe or the break-up of the European Union. The 12 per cent most in favour would like to keep up the momentum of integration while the 12 per cent least in favour think it has gone too far.

A lack of support for further movement towards an ever closer Union does not imply opposition to the EU as it is. When asked whether EU membership is a good thing or bad thing for their country, 63 per cent of EES respondents are positive about the status quo. However, it is wrong to assume that those who favour the EU as it is want more integration on principle. Among those viewing their country's membership positively, only half also endorse further integration; the other half prefer to leave the EU as it is. In other words, even people who approve their country being a member of the EU as it is today are as likely to be against further integration as in favour of it. Moreover, the intensification of economic problems associated with the euro crisis threatens the maintenance of majority satisfaction.

When heads of national governments endorse further integration in meetings of the European Council they do not represent the views of most of their citizens. There is no national majority in favour of further integration in 23 of 27 member states and in five states there is a plurality against. As long as heads of government saw themselves as trustees for the national interest, they had no hesitation in taking decisions beyond what public opinion favoured. Governors assumed that the indifferent middle mass would passively accept their lead. EU leadership now requires a different approach. When there are visible costs that are high in impact, national governors cannot expect their citizens to go along passively with steps towards a closer Union. Instead, to convince the critical group of citizens who are neither pro nor anti European, advocates of policies leading to more integration must make a pragmatic case that justifies each step forward on its own merits.

3

A Union of Diverse Peoples

Whoever speaks of Europe is wrong; it is a geographical expression.

Otto von Bismarck, Prussian Prime Minister

We have made Europe. Now we must make Europeans.

After Massimo d'Azeglio

A state has fixed boundaries; the European Union does not. It has intentionally been constructed with indefinite boundaries. In this it is true to Europe's past, for the political boundaries of Europe have never been fixed. Empires and states could and did come and go. Until the end of the First World War, Tsarist Russia and the Ottoman Empire were part of Europe. In 1957 overseas colonies of France were represented in its national Parliament and remained 'European' until they gained independence. By contrast, although Britain had a national interest in preventing a single country from dominating the European continent, it used sea power to protect it from the continent and create an Empire that linked it with continents that were oceans away.

Europe has always been a continent of diverse peoples but diversity has never been an obstacle to political union. To strengthen alliances or gain territory, monarchies arranged dynastic marriages that created the multi-national empires that dominated Europe before 1914. The Austro-Hungarian Empire was an extreme example of diversity, for the majority of peoples living under the Habsburg crown were neither Austrians nor Hungarians. However, nationalist movements led to the break-up of multi-national empires. After the First World War, new nation-states were created that emphasized ethnic exclusivity, even when they had large minority populations and Germany under Adolf Hitler sought continental domination claiming to represent a *Herrenvolk* (master race). The Second World War discredited claims to national superiority while the Holocaust and the displacement of minorities increased the ethnic homogeneity of European states.

The cosmopolitan founders of the European Union wanted to create a new political institution that rejected nationalism. Even so fervent a French patriot as General Charles de Gaulle saw co-operation with other European countries as desirable, since it offered a means of defending France against defeat in yet another European war. The European Union was founded without any pretence that the peoples of the six founder states constituted a single nation. Nor did the elite process of building an ever closer Union require the mass of the population to identify themselves as Europeans.

The EU's diversity is officially recognized in documents that describe in the plural the nations and peoples of Europe. The primary citizenship of Europeans is national citizenship. European citizenship is an add-on that half a billion people, including the EU's strongest critics, acquire without asking for it. Although every EU member must be a democratic state, there is great diversity in how long they have been democratic. The eight North European countries that are old democracies are a minority of EU member states. A majority of states have applied for admission to the EU not long after a democratic regime replaced an undemocratic one. This group includes ten post-Communist countries plus Greece, Portugal, and Spain. Three EU founder states—Germany, Italy, and France—alternated between democratic and undemocratic regimes until after the Second World War.

Language is the best example of diversity. When the European Union was founded, it had four official languages; today it has 23 languages—and is committed to adding to this number as more countries join. With less than half the population of India, the world's largest and most linguistically fragmented democracy, the EU has far more official languages. The number is now so large that most political communication within the EU is carried out by people speaking a foreign language.

In the past half century developments in television, telecommunications, and cheap air travel have made national borders much weaker barriers to the trans-national diffusion of common influences, often described as Europeanization. It affects leisure-time activities, such as pop music, holidays, and football competitions. Consumer goods now carry labels in half a dozen languages. Workers in national firms must compete with what is produced in other parts of Europe and multi-national firms define the world in terms of markets not states. Friendships and family ties among people from different countries are forged through peaceful contacts rather than the exigencies of war. EU policies consciously encourage this process, for example, through programmes promoting student mobility and such symbols as the EU flag. However, the power of symbols depends on the institutions that they represent. The reproduction on euro notes of classic European architecture such as Greek temples and Roman aqueducts is no substitute for national economies built on solid foundations.

The opening up of national societies to other European countries has been happening in parallel with globalization, an increase in the movement of people, goods, and ideas across continents. EU policies have encouraged the integration of Europe into a global economy in which automobiles can have European, American, or Japanese names on the outside and on the inside engines that combine parts from multiple continents. For people who are nationally oriented, there may be little distinction between Europeanization, Americanization, and globalization. All these terms refer to forces that exist 'out there', beyond the culture with which they are familiar and often beyond the reach of their national government.

It is a fallacy of methodological nationalism to assume that national statistics apply equally to every citizen. Within every society average income statistics mask differences between high- and low-income groups. Social divisions found within a society, for example, between young and old, have the potential to create links between people across national boundaries. The unemployed in France and Germany may have more in common with each other than with fellow-nationals who are bankers, and well educated people can be more at home in a cosmopolitan environment than with less educated people with whom they share national citizenship.

Cross-national activities have not created a homogeneous European society. Politics cannot be reduced to what people eat or watch on television. The European Union is not a nation-state in which people who share a common identity have come together to create a new political authority. Nor is it a 'state-nation', like the United States, in which political institutions create a national identity common to peoples of diverse origins. Contrary to many academic theories, European identification has not been a condition of European integration nor has Europeanization of identities replaced stealth as the motive force for an ever closer Union. A European outlook is neither a necessary nor a sufficient condition for greater integration. If it had been, the EU would not have achieved the extent of integration it has reached today.

I Enlargement Across a Continent

At its foundation the European Union was not representative of historic Europe. It had less than one-fifth the land area of what a nineteenth-century monarch would have recognized as Europe. The Iron Curtain was no metaphor, but a barrier cutting through the historic lands of Central Europe, most starkly in the division of Germany into two states. In doing so, it created two Europes. The states of Western Europe were democratic and had prospering market economies; the Communist states of Eastern Europe were undemocratic and their economies were burdened by the dictates of Moscow.

The founder states of the European Union were determined to keep open the possibility of more countries joining. The 1957 Treaty of Rome stated, 'Any European state may apply to become a member of the Community', a form of words that leaves open what the boundaries of Europe are. It gives any state the opportunity to put forward an application to join on its own initiative, while leaving members free to make decisions about whether it meets EU standards for admission. The first step in EU membership is that an applicant country's credentials are examined to see whether it is ready to be a candidate. Morocco is the only country that has been told it was ineligible to apply for EU membership because it is not European. Once a country becomes a formal candidate for membership, it is subject to a detailed examination by Commission officials to determine whether it has the institutional capacity to meet the obligations of EU membership. For the most part, this involves questions of the consistency of national laws and administrative practices with those of member states. Acceptance of a candidate as a member requires the unanimous consent of existing member states. No candidate country has been refused admission, but some have been kept waiting indefinitely.

Consolidating Western Europe. The anxiety of non-member states about the costs of being left out of the EEC led to the founding of the European Free Trade Association (EFTA) in 1960. It allowed free trade in industrial goods between EFTA and EEC member states without subjecting the former to the political obligations of EEC membership. The seven charter members of EFTA were Britain, Austria, Denmark, Norway, Portugal, Sweden, and Switzerland. Five have since become EU members. Although the Norwegian government twice agreed to join the EU, Norway's voters rejected their government's decision in referendums. Decisions of the Swiss government to have closer EU ties have likewise been rejected in referendums. Today, the EFTA half-way house is nearly vacant. In addition to Norway and Switzerland, the only other members are Iceland and Liechtenstein.

The first enlargement of the EU in 1973 increased the EU's capacity to act for the free and prosperous nations of Europe. Britain, Denmark, and Ireland were older democracies than three major founder states and had established market economies. Before this group could be admitted, it was necessary to overcome both British and French resistance to the idea that Britain belonged in Europe. This enlargement round filled the gap left by Britain's unwillingness to be a founder EU member state and by Charles de Gaulle's initial unwillingness to dilute French influence by admitting Britain.

Democracy was made a condition of membership when two members of NATO, Franco's Spain and Salazar's Portugal, made approaches about joining.

Committed democrats in the founder states secured the rebuff of both because they then lacked democratic institutions. When the military established a dictatorship in Greece, arrangements for an association agreement were suspended. Making democracy a necessary condition for membership left the door open for a country to re-apply as and when it became a new democracy. By the late 1970s all three countries had exchanged their rebuffed regimes for democratic institutions and Greece, Spain, and Portugal became EU members in the 1980s. These additions increased the EU's Mediterranean links.

Achieving continental scope. The fall of the Berlin Wall in 1989 transformed the map of Europe. Since the Soviet Union could no longer threaten sanctions if countries abandoned their formal neutrality between east and west, Austria, Finland, and Sweden could and did become EU members. In states freed from subservience to Moscow by the collapse of Communism, new governments were eager to join the European Union as a guarantee that their freedom would be maintained. However, their political institutions and economies had been modelled on Soviet rather than European practices. Moreover, with the exception of Czechoslovakia, dictatorship had previously been the political norm in Eastern Europe.

Because of the flood of membership applications after the fall of the Berlin Wall, at a meeting in Copenhagen in 1993 the EU set out five criteria for admission: a democratic form of government, respect for human rights and minorities, adherence to the rule of law, effective public administration, and a functioning market economy. The criteria mix political values, good government standards, and requirements of the single European market. Each is clear in principle but broad enough to allow applicant countries freedom to decide what kind of political institutions to adopt. For most applicant states, the chief models for emulation have been the Federal Republic of Germany and Sweden. All applicants are also expected to adopt laws that implement the obligations of the *acquis communautaire*.

All the post-Communist states seeking admission had economic problems arising from the legacy of non-market Soviet-style economies that could not compete with normal West European economies. All the states also had administrative and legal structures that had been distorted by subservience to the authority of the Communist Party. The EU financed technical assistance to applicants, for example, training government statisticians accustomed to making up statistics for a non-market economy to compile statistics acceptable to the EU's statistical office. Some raised awkward political issues. Particular problems arose in Slovakia as long as it had a prime minister, Vladimir Meciar, who showed dictatorial inclinations. In Estonia and Latvia the status of a large minority of Russian non-citizens who had been moved there in Soviet times was queried by Brussels. Poland, the only populous East European state, pressed claims to voting rights that were deemed excessive by other big states.

The decision about admitting a country is caught up in asymmetries of power. The EU is powerful because the desire of applicants to join makes them predisposed to accept EU conditions for gaining entry. However, an asymmetry of knowledge benefits applicant countries. They know far better than officials in Brussels how their institutions actually work. In the process of discussing the requirements of the *acquis*, national officials learn 'Eurospeak', that is, the terminology that EU institutions use when evaluating countries for membership. They also learn how to get around problems that could cause their application for membership to stall.

Since candidate countries usually have member states sponsoring them, the Commission officials making evaluations are under pressure to be optimistic about progress towards meeting the Copenhagen criteria. If evidence is in short supply, an applicant can appeal for admission on the grounds that this would have a 'Europeanizing' effect, that is, help it meet conditions for membership after joining. However, an intensive analysis of the effects of EU enlargement on post-Communist countries concludes that the influence of conditionality is a myth.[1]

After considering a staggered enlargement with the best qualified post-Communist applicants admitted first, the EU went for a big bang approach. In 2004 eight post-Communist countries were admitted—the Czech Republic, Estonia, Hungary, Latvia, Lithuania, Poland, Slovakia, and Slovenia—plus Cyprus and Malta. When this happened, the Czech prime minister spoke for tens of millions of the living and many millions more who had perished when he said, 'This is the end of World War Two.' After Bulgaria and Romania gave commitments to continue upgrading their political systems following admission, they became member states in 2007. Croatia is scheduled to be admitted in July 2013. The delay in its admission was not due to a low level of development. In 2011 Croatia's Gross Domestic Product per capita was higher than that of six member states and its Transparency International Corruption rating was better than that of four EU member states. Entry was delayed because of the effects of Croatia's involvement in war following the break-up of the Republic of Yugoslavia.

Enlargement has made Europe more than a geographical expression; 95 per cent of the continent's population is now part of the European Union. At the same time, new members have increased the EU's internal diversity and brought with it new neighbours. In the east the EU now extends from the Baltic to the Black Sea. Its neighbours are Russia, Belarus, Ukraine, Moldova, and Turkey. The island of Cyprus is closer to Syria and Lebanon than it is to Greece. The admission of Croatia will give the EU borders with Bosnia & Herzegovina, Serbia, and Montenegro. On the Atlantic side of Europe, the ocean links Ireland with Boston, and Portugal with Brazil.

II Differentiating Member States

Enlargement has changed the political shape of the European Union. The European Union is no longer a league of West European countries with Paris at its centre. Instead, *Mitteleuropa*, the old German term for Central Europe, is once again central in European politics. Berlin, rather than Paris or Bonn, is now the most important national capital in Europe. The great increase in the number of member states has made building consensus in EU institutions more complicated. European Council members can no longer meet around a table suitable for discussion in a private house and there is not time to listen at length to the views of the head of each national government. Juridical equality gives even the smallest state the privilege of holding important EU positions such as the Presidency of the Council of Ministers, which rotates between member states every six months.

A Union of 27 states is certain to have more diversity than a Union of six countries. Yet the greater the number of member states, the more difficult it is to characterize every country in terms of unique features. Whatever attribute is examined, the typical pattern is that member states cluster together in groups with which they share important features that differentiate them from other states. For example, there is a cluster of countries bordering the Atlantic where fishing is important, and a cluster of landlocked members. Similarly, there is a cluster of wine-growing countries and a cluster where beer and spirits are the national drinks. The Benelux and Nordic states have political and administrative institutions to look after common interests while countries such as Ireland and Portugal have no such alliance.

Clustering rejects the extreme nationalist assertion that every European country is completely different from every other country. It also rejects the extreme rhetorical claim that all Europeans share common values and interests. Because no country is unique in all its characteristics, each is likely to have allies when one of its interests is affected by EU policies. Because clusters of countries differ, bargaining and compromise are required to arrive at a consensus of diverse countries.

Sizing up member states. The common characteristic of belonging to the European Union does not make its member states equal in resources useful for political influence. Differences in population affect the number of votes that a country has in the European Parliament and in the Council of Ministers. A second resource, money, depends on both the size of a country's total Gross Domestic Product and on the per capita value of its GDP. Thus, Poland has a much bigger total GDP than Finland, but Finns have a much higher income per head. A third resource, the extent to which a government acts corruptly, reflects national variations in commitment to the rule of law (Table 3.1).

Table 3.1. Economy, population, and corruption

	GDP		Population		Corruption	
	per cap €	Index	(mns)	Index	Rating	Index
	Index value of 100 represents median country					
Luxembourg	82,700	376	0.511	5	8.5	137
Denmark	43,100	196	5.560	59	9.4	152
Sweden	41,000	186	9.415	100	9.3	150
Netherlands	36,100	164	16.654	177	8.9	143
Austria	35,800	163	8.355	89	7.8	126
Finland	35,600	162	5.375	57	9.4	152
Ireland	34,900	159	4.480	48	7.5	121
Belgium	33,500	152	10.918	116	7.5	121
Germany	31,400	143	81.751	868	8.0	129
France	29,900	136	65.075	691	7.0	113
United Kingdom	27,700	126	62.435	663	7.8	126
Italy	26,000	118	60.626	644	3.9	63
Spain	23,300	106	46.152	490	6.2	100
Cyprus	22,000	100	0.804	8	6.3	102
Greece	19,000	86	11.329	120	3.4	55
Slovenia	17,400	79	2.050	22	5.9	95
Portugal	16,100	73	10.636	113	6.1	98
Malta	15,300	69	0.417	4	5.6	90
Czech Rep	14,700	67	10.532	112	4.4	71
Slovakia	12,700	58	5.435	58	4.0	64
Estonia	11,900	54	1.340	14	6.4	103
Hungary	10,100	46	9.986	106	4.6	74
Latvia	9,700	44	2.229	24	4.2	68
Lithuania	9,500	43	3.244	34	4.8	77
Poland	9,300	42	38.200	406	5.5	89
Romania	5,800	26	21.413	227	3.6	58
Bulgaria	4,800	22	7.504	80	3.3	53

Source: GDP per capita in euros, Eurostat 2011, <http://appsso.eurostat.ec.europa.eu/nui/show.do?dataset=nama_gdp_c&lang=en>
Population as of 1 January 2011. Corruption Index from Transparency International at <http://www. transparency.org>.

Differences in population are extreme; Germany has a population almost 200 times that of Malta. However, the enlargement of the European Union has diminished Germany's share of the EU's total population. In 1957 Germany had almost 30 per cent of the EU's population. After re-unification in 1990 increased its population by one-quarter, Germany had more than one-fifth of the population of a 15-member Union. However, following the increase in the EU's population with enlargement, Germany's proportion of the EU population has fallen to one-sixth of the total. Four states—Germany, France, Britain, and Italy—are conventionally bracketed together as big states and the population of Spain and Poland gives each a substantial number of votes in the European Parliament and Council of Ministers. Only two states, Romania and the Netherlands, are medium size.

The population of most EU member states ranges from small to very small. Among the EU's member states, Sweden, with 9.4 million people, has the median population. The population of the largest small state, Greece, is more than two and one-half times that of the smallest small state, Malta. The 19 smaller states divide into three sub-categories: small (8 countries with populations from 7 to 12 million); smaller (8 countries with 1 to 6 million people); and tiny (3 countries with less than one million population).

Within a single European market, the absolute size of a country's Gross Domestic Product is important. Germany's Gross Domestic Product is hundreds of times larger than that of most small states, because it is both prosperous and populous. Equally important, its GDP is also up to a third larger than that of Europe's three other largest states and more than ten times that of the GDP of the median EU economy, Finland. Even though the average Finn enjoys a high standard of individual income, the country's economic importance is lowered by its small population.

The disparity between the average income of citizens in EU member states is very far from the EU's goal of social cohesion, which calls for limited income differences between countries. However, this has not been achieved. Although every country has tended to see its average national income rise from one decade to the next, big differences in starting points maintain diversity in living standards. Among older EU member states, the Gross Domestic Product per capita of Portugal is less than two-fifths that of Denmark. Differences between older and new member states are much greater, because the latter suffer the persisting effects of having had Soviet-style non-market economies. After almost a decade of EU membership, the GDP per capita of Bulgaria is only one-eighth that of Denmark, and nine of the ten formerly Communist economies still have a lower standard of living than Portugal.

Notwithstanding the EU requirement that all states should respect the rule of law, there are great differences in the extent to which they do so. Differences are especially great among older EU member states. Nordic countries are among the most honest in the world, with ratings above 9 on the 10-point Transparency International Corruption Perceptions Index. However, Italy and Greece have ratings below 4, placing them lower than ten new EU member states and closer to the level of corruption in the developing world. Since EU laws and cash grants are administered by officials of national governments, the extent to which a regime is honest or corrupt immediately affects how much benefit and who benefits from the money that the EU provides.

When countries are grouped according to their national prosperity and integrity, there are four clusters. Almost half of EU countries are *economically prosperous and honest* in their system of governance. Populous countries such as Germany and France as well as small countries such as Luxembourg and Ireland are in this group. Almost all these countries are older EU member states. Estonia and Slovenia show that it is possible to be *honest although not so prosperous*; their avoidance of corruption meets the EU average even though their economies do not have the per capita income of the median member, Cyprus. Italy has the dubious distinction of being deviant, since it is relatively *prosperous but not honest*. The effect of the Communist legacy on national integrity as well as the national economy is shown by the number of new member states, led by Bulgaria and Romania, which are *neither prosperous nor honest*. Four others have a GDP per capita less than half that of the median EU country and are also negatively rated on the Corruption Perceptions Index. Greece is the only older EU member state to be on the margins of this group, since its per capita income is low by standards of older member states and its integrity is low by the standards of new member states.

III Mass Reactions to Europeanization

The great social, economic, and political changes that have taken place in European societies since the EU was founded are undeniable. However, their causes and political consequences are problematic. Up to a point, these changes can be ascribed to Europeanization, that is, an increase in the movement of people, goods, and ideas across national boundaries, and the European Union has significantly contributed to this.

Whether and how people respond to Europeanization reflects individual circumstances. Exposure need not be linked with the European Union. For example, the Union of European Football Associations (UEFA) was established before the EU and the 53 countries that compete are divided almost equally between countries that are EU members and those that are not. European citizens may be more interested in how well their favourite football team represents them in UEFA competitions than how well their prime minister represents them in Brussels. Nor do contacts with foreigners necessarily lead to positive responses. If a holiday abroad involves unfavourable experiences, then tourists may project their negative feelings onto Europe as a whole.

To assume a uniform response to Europeanization ignores the extent to which differences of income, education, and age found in every member state may affect reactions to other countries, thus creating differences even among those who are exposed to Europeanization. The conventional assumption is that the more cosmopolitan an individual becomes, the more he or she will support European integration, because it provides institutional underpinnings for cosmopolitan contacts across the continent. Those who are not Europeanized are assumed to have their political values unaffected. However, this ignores the extent to which there are losers as well as winners from change, such as workers who lose their job because their employer shifts production to another country and those who resent their neighbourhood having immigrants from other countries. The creation of losers through increased Europeanization can make it a salient issue and put pressure on their national government to do something about the national consequences of changes in the world out there.

Persisting economic divisions within national borders. There is an important half-truth in the claim that the citizens of Europe share many common interests and values. While the same views can be found in all EU member states, it is wrong to infer that all Europeans share the same values and interests. Each national society is divided socially and economically. Insofar as within-country differences are paralleled in other countries, this can strengthen cross-national agreement. For example, trade union members may hold similar views whatever their nationality and the same can be true of employers. Although the members of the EU's Economic and Social Committee are appointed by national governments, they sit as representatives of multi-national groups of employers, employees, or civil society organizations. Likewise, in the European Parliament MEPs vote as members of multi-national Party Groups.

A democratic society recognizes many social differences but does not politicize them, as happens in a political system with totalitarian institutions. The EU's Copenhagen criteria of standards that political institutions ought to meet is mute about political cleavages within its member states. However, political sociologists theorize that economic divisions in a society create solidarity among people in the same class. The Eurozone crisis has very visibly shown the importance of trans-national influences on national economies. It has also demonstrated divisions at the EU level between those who believe that priority should be given to fighting inflation and those who put economic growth first.

The European Quality of Life Survey asks a battery of questions about the extent to which people see a variety of social differences creating tensions in their society. While few see a lot of tension between men and women or young and old, economic tensions are substantial. An average of 30 per cent say there is a lot of tension between rich and poor and 32 per cent report a lot of tension between management and workers. Tensions tend to be higher in new member states, where differences between Communist apparatchiks and the masses have been replaced by those between major beneficiaries of the transition to a market economy and those who feel left behind. In Hungary as many as 71 per cent feel a lot of tension between rich and poor and 63 per cent feel a lot of tension between management and workers. By contrast, less than 10 per cent in Scandinavian countries and less than one in five Britons see class differences as important.[2]

Equality of citizenship does not get rid of inequalities of income. Differences between average incomes of EU member states are paralleled by differences in income within each member state. Every society in Europe is divided between above average, average, and below average income groups. To compare the extent of income inequality between member states, Eurostat calculates a Gini Index of inequality of income. Compared to a theoretical value of 0.00 for complete income equality and 1.00 for total inequality, in 2010 the mean Gini Index for EU countries was 0.31. There is very little difference between national societies in the degree of income inequality; four-fifths cluster within five points of the mean. The least income inequality is found in Slovenia and Sweden, where the Gini Index is 0.24, and the most in Lithuania, which has a Gini Index of 0.37. Concern about income inequality divides Europeans into those who see themselves as losers rather than winners. At the time of the 2009 EES survey, 58 per cent of Europeans favoured the redistribution of income, against 23 per cent disagreeing and a fifth having no opinion.

Although the global economic crisis has had an impact on every European country, each society continues to be divided between households that have no difficulty in paying their bills, those having occasional problems, and a minority having chronic problems. The autumn 2011 Eurobarometer survey found that while there was overwhelmingly agreement that national governments faced big economic difficulties, 61 per cent judged the financial situation of their household as fairly or very good as against 36 per cent assessing it as fairly bad or very bad. The proportion satisfied with their economic condition ranged between 90 per cent in Sweden and 24 per cent in Greece. In effect, the global economic crisis has not altered a major feature of European societies: earnings and welfare state benefits shelter the majority from economic difficulties while a minority has a chronic problem of making ends meet.

Socialization into a wider world. Europeanization encourages individuals to think beyond the boundaries of their own country. It creates conditions for the development of a public sphere in which Europeans of different nationalities may communicate about European politics. However, many European public spaces are not politically relevant. An airport hall with people of dozens of nationalities is not a place for political dialogue. Even when European awareness increases, this need not produce commitment to an ever closer Union. Campaigners against European integration give a lot of attention to what happens in Brussels.

The single Europe market has Europeanized what virtually every family consumes. Supermarket shelves carry goods labelled in multiple European languages so that producers do not need separate packages to meet common tastes. It is the exception rather than the rule for the EU to allow products to trademark their origin. When this happens it usually refers to a city or region, such as Parma ham or Scotch whisky, rather than to a member state. Products such as computers contain parts from a multiplicity of countries. The openness of the EU to global free trade facilitates the import of cheap goods from other continents. What one buys and eats need not affect political attitudes. People who buy television sets made in Asia are not expressing a desire for political union with China any more than Germans who buy Italian shoes are endorsing their country joining the Republic of Italy.

The Europeanization of consumption is now a banal fact of life that people can benefit from without knowing the European Union's role in making this possible. Travellers do not need to be aware of the EU promotion of airline competition to book a cheap flight to a holiday abroad. Upwards of half of Europeans annually take a holiday in another country, typically a country in the Mediterranean such as Spain. The political effect of holidaying abroad tends to be limited. People do not go to beach resorts in order to sit in their hotel room viewing another country's political news on television and a bad experience in a holiday hotel can turn people against their fellow European citizens.

The single Europe market has made knowing a foreign language vocationally useful. Given that Europeans have dozens of home languages, this has created the demand for a *lingua franca*, that is, a language that can be used to communicate in many different countries. In the EU of six countries that language was French. Today English is the usual language of communication between two Europeans who do not have the same home language. More than three-quarters of Europeans knowing English are not British. English as a Foreign Language (EFL) is a tool to facilitate trans-national communication. Even though only one per cent of Eurozone citizens are native English speakers, it is the language in which the German-based European Central Bank debates what to do about the euro. It does not confer 'soft' power on Britain nor does it encourage Britain's governors to engage and seek to understand the points of view of other European countries. Even less does it give Washington power over Europe.

A European identity? The European Commission actively promotes a European identity in the belief that this will create support for an ever closer Union, just as the development of national identities played a part in creating nation-states. It sponsors programmes to encourage positive awareness of what the EU does and encourages trans-national personal contacts through twinning arrangements between cities and towns in different EU countries. Each year several cities are selected as European cities of culture. The total cost of public relations efforts of the Commission and the Parliament is several billion euros a year.

A treaty can create European citizens but this does not mean that people immediately think of themselves as Europeans. Conferring European citizenship on almost half a billion people is legally significant. However, the psychological impact is limited, since individuals do not apply to become EU citizens nor do they have to pass a test on the meaning of being a European. Whereas American citizenship can be achieved only if one passes a test about the United States, European citizenship is automatically conferred on anyone who is a citizen of an EU member state.

The European Union has promoted a blue flag with a circle of gold stars as its brand symbol. Its image is at airport passport controls, on local government buildings receiving grants from Brussels and on drivers' licences, and it may appear on national passports. Pro-EU national governments display the flag along with their national flag to show solidarity with Europe. For example, two towers of the Berlin building that houses the German Parliament fly the German flag and two fly the flag of the European Union. When a 2007 Eurobarometer survey showed people a picture of the EU flag without a label, 95 per cent said that they had seen it. However, this was not followed up with a question about whether they knew what it represented; that could have shown an embarrassing amount of ignorance. Instead, respondents were told it was an EU flag. Thus prompted, 54 per cent said they identified with the flag while 46 per cent did not.

Consistent with Europe's multi-level system of government, public opinion surveys ask people whether they have a national identity, a European identity, or some combination of both. More than nine-tenths give priority to their national identity on its own or as their primary identity. Two in five exclusively identify with their state and almost half put their national identity ahead of a secondary identification with Europe (Figure 3.1). The percentage

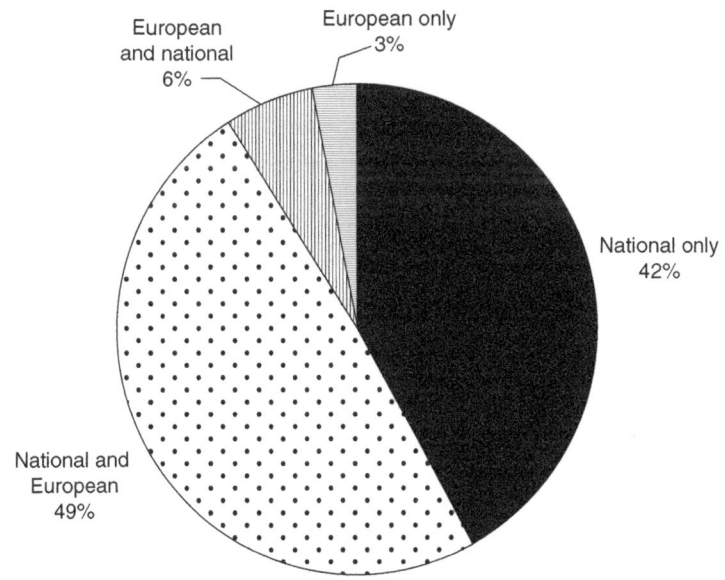

Figure 3.1. National identity and European identity

Source: European Election Survey, 2009. Number of respondents in 27 countries: 27,069.

giving exclusive priority to their national identity is highest in Britain, 67 per cent. The proportion identifying solely with their country has tended to remain steady over the decades. By contrast, only 3 per cent identify solely with Europe and 6 per cent place European identification ahead of national identification.

The development of a secondary identification with Europe among almost half of Europe's citizens has resulted in a new cultural division within member states. In addition to people dividing along nationality lines such as British, French, Germans, and Italians, there is now a division among citizens of a country between people who think of themselves solely in terms of their national identity and those who have at least a secondary identification with Europe.

Europeanization without further integration. Theories of Europeanization tend to assume that the more people know about the European Union, the more they should favour integration. From this perspective, not supporting the EU is a consequence of a lack of knowledge rather than informed rejection. Europe's citizens are divided almost equally among those with some or little or no knowledge of the Union that has given them citizenship. In reply to three EES questions testing knowledge of the European Union, an average of 55 per cent gave correct answers. However, there is only a three percentage point difference in support for further integration between those with know-ledge of the EU and those without it. In other words, support for integration is a minority view among those who identify with Europe and those who do not. This is not surprising in view of the finding of a 2012 Eurobarometer survey that the two features most frequently linked with European identity have conflicting implications: 45 per cent see Europe as about democracy and freedom while 43 per cent identify Europe with the euro.

Since the European Union is very complex and relatively remote, more educated people ought to be able to make more informed judgements about it. This is sometimes voiced by non-elected EU policymakers as a justification for acting as trustees for the common good of Europe rather than sharing major decisions with less informed citizens. While education reduces the percentage of those who answer don't know to questions about the European Union, more educated people are not especially strong supporters of an ever closer Union. At all levels of education, the median group prefers leaving the EU as it is, and the most educated are just as likely as the least educated to think that integration has gone too far.

Since more and more of the EU's citizens have been born after their country became an EU member, the turnover of generations could increase support for integration, as an increasing part of Europe's population will have been socialized to think of the EU as a given part of their system of governance. However, there is a limited difference between young and old in attitudes

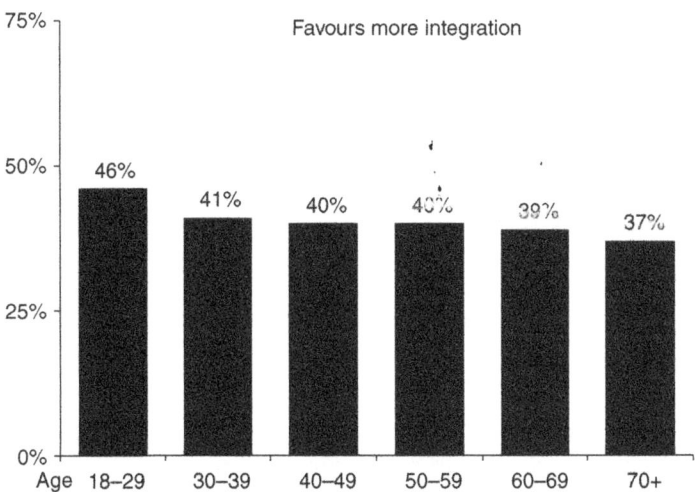

Figure 3.2. Support for European integration by age groups

Source: European Election Survey, 2009. Number of respondents in 27 countries: 27,069.

toward European integration. Among Europeans age 18 to 29, 46 per cent favour more integration while among those age 70 or above, 37 per cent do so (Figure 3.2). This difference does not mean that older people are more likely to think integration has gone too far; it reflects older people being readier to endorse the status quo than are younger Europeans.

The most optimistic extrapolation in favour of an ever closer Union is that it would take at least 30 years for the turnover of generations to make pro-Europeans a majority. However, within a country, national opinion about European integration tends to be stable. Thus, any forecast about the turnover of generations should be stamped with the familiar statistical health warning 'all other conditions remaining equal'. The failure is striking of a half century of Europeanization to produce majority support for an ever closer Union. The deepening and broadening of EU policies have not only increased EU awareness but also sustained disagreement about whether more of the same is desirable or integration has gone too far.

4

Citizenship Lite

The Union will no longer be judged solely by its ability to remove barriers to trade or to complete an internal market; its legitimacy today depends on involvement and participation.

European Commission White Paper on European Governance

All governments limit who or what they represent; they differ in where they draw the line. The European Union is a union of states; there is nothing new in this. International treaties have always been agreements between states not peoples. The 1815 Congress of Vienna was a compact between monarchies represented by aristocrats and diplomats, and citizens of UN member states differ greatly in their rights. The limitation of EU membership to democratic states and a Parliament that is elected makes the European Union substantially more democratic than conventional international organizations. However, member states have consistently rejected the idea that it should give primacy to the rights of its citizens rather than its member states.

The EU's unique political system does not conform to that of its member states. The European Commission is encouraged to engage in continuing horizontal dialogues with other EU institutions but also with Brussels-based organizations of economic and social interests affected by EU policies. They contribute information and political support relevant to the adoption and implementation of what the Commission proposes and the Commission draws on this when putting proposals forward for approval by the Council of Ministers and the European Parliament. When issues arise of broad public interest, such as gender discrimination, the Commission invites participation by many groups that are advocates of causes. However, because they are not elected it is difficult to determine who or what these groups actually represent.

Vertical consultation through EU institutions directly connected to citizens is limited. The members of the Convention called to draft a Constitution to link Europe's citizens more closely with the EU's goals were selected rather than elected. Within the Constitutional Convention there was a consensus about what should be done and national governments endorsed a Constitution. However, when citizens were consulted in national referendums, it turned out that governments that had approved the Constitution did not necessarily represent a majority of their citizens.

The EU offers citizenship lite, because the rights that people have as European citizens are much less than their rights as national citizens. Like non-alcoholic beer, citizenship lite appears to be a contradiction in terms. It reflects the contradiction between the EU's desire to claim democratic credentials and the way in which its institutions actually operate. The Treaty of the European Union proclaims that every citizen has the right to participate in the political life of the Union. However, when the Commission published a report on *Dismantling the Obstacles to EU Citizens' Rights* in 2010, the primary emphasis was on measures to help people transfer their employment, car insurance, or pensions from one country to the other. It assumed that the chief political obstacle facing individual participation was a lack of information about how the EU works rather than a lack of institutions by which citizens could hold the EU to account.[1]

Today's need for popular commitment to policies with visible costs challenges the European Union to strengthen its procedures for consulting the people it nominally represents. The challenge is pragmatic as well as normative. People can, in their role as national citizens, reject commitments that their national government has entered into in Brussels.

I National Governments Pulled Two Ways

In Europe's multi-dimensional political system, national governments are at the intersection of conflicting horizontal and vertical pressures. In domestic politics, a government is accountable to its national electorate. Within the European Council, prime ministers are subject to a horizontal pull from colleagues with whom they are jointly responsible for EU decisions. The Eurozone crisis has made very evident the strains on national leaders being pulled two ways. Because Germany is financially the strongest member of the Eurozone, the German Chancellor has had to reconcile electoral accountability to a coalition government, to the *Bundestag*, and to the German Federal Court with responsibilities to other Eurozone governments. Concurrently, Greek prime ministers have struggled to gain support from the Greek electorate and parliament for measures that the EU insists are necessary conditions of funding the current costs of Greece's past financial and political profligacy.

Since major EU policies require endorsement by popularly elected national governments meeting in the European Council, the EU can claim to consult the peoples of Europe indirectly. However, national governments are not elected to agree decisions in Brussels. They are elected to take decisions nationally. In national politics politicians share a common fate: they are accountable to the same parliament and electorate. Parliamentary debates and the media give Opposition politicians lots of opportunities to demonstrate that there is no consensus about what the national government is doing. Opinion polls and the media provide continuous reminders to governors of the threat of defeat at the next national election. Because competitive elections are an integral part of democracy, competing views on policy are normal in national politics, including views about what the government's position ought to be on major issues that face the European Union as a whole.

A fundamental change takes place when a national prime minister switches from chairing a national Cabinet to sitting in a European Council meeting with 26 other prime ministers. Instead of being in charge of policymaking, she or he is one among many participants in complicated multi-lateral negotiations. In both national and EU institutions the object is to agree a policy. However, the means of doing so are different. In the European Council each national prime minister must co-operate with governments subject to different electorates; otherwise, the EU cannot take any action. The incentive to agree on problems too big to be dealt with at the national level is that an EU policy may be beneficial to the country that the prime minister represents. However, participants often differ on national or partisan lines about what specifically the EU should do. Bargaining is necessary to arrive at a consensus about policy. The choice facing a national prime minister is between accepting a package of compromises, even if only a second-best solution in national terms, or presenting demands that fail to influence the consensus that is arrived at and having to defend nationally an outcome that is a lesser or even greater evil.

A government pulled two ways can try to appease its national constituency by speaking against a proposal but not voting against it. It can make a dissenting statement while abstaining from casting a negative vote. A dissenting statement can be publicized domestically as evidence that the government has presented views popular at home. However, such 'constructive abstention' does not prevent the approval of major measures. Any short-term benefit that a government gains by fighting a losing battle in Brussels is soon lost in national politics. However, the measure it opposed remains in place as part of the EU's *acquis*.

European Union policies cannot be agreed simply on the basis of national interests, for that would produce an endless sequence of national vetoes. Its policies are meant to express a European interest that is unlikely to match exactly the interests of all 27 member states. In the compromises arising from bargaining within the Council, each national government is required to make concessions about its national interest in order to achieve a multi-national consensus on policies in the collective interest of Europe.

In the European Parliament, each country is represented by different national parties that tend to favour competing views of what is in the interest of their national electorate, while in the European Council and Council of Ministers each national government, even though elected by only half of its citizens, makes commitments that bind the country as a whole, not only for its own term of office but also for the terms of its successors. The doctrine that foreign policy is about national interests is often used to justify making commitments on behalf of the entire country. Insofar as issues are about what EU policy should be towards problems in other continents, a national government may enjoy passive consent from its citizens. However, as the national impact of EU policies has increased, it tends to face bigger issues that are both visible and controversial domestically. A prime minister can tell colleagues in the European Council about domestic difficulties with an EU policy, but this may not produce concessions from other prime ministers who face political difficulties at home too.

Each state's representative in the Council must speak with a single voice and its votes are cast as a bloc. However, each national government represents only a fraction of a country's citizens (Figure 4.1). At the time of the latest European Parliament election, only two national governments, those of Austria and Germany, could claim to speak for at least two-thirds of their electorate. This was because each was governed by a grand coalition of the country's two largest parties. Ten more governments were backed by at least half their nation's voters. Given the bonus that electoral systems award big parties, a majority of national governments at Council meetings represent a minority of their country's voters. Three governments held office with the support of less than two-fifths of their voters, including the extreme case of the Labour government in Britain, which represented only 35 per cent of the country's voters. Such statistics place a question mark over a national government's claim to represent the whole of its country in deliberations in Brussels. This is especially true of countries where there is a politically vocal party opposing European integration.

Because national electoral calendars are not co-ordinated with European Parliament elections, there is no assurance that a national government will be supported by the same parties as those with a majority of the country's MEPs. In a European Parliament election, voters may cast a ballot as a mid-term protest against their government's domestic policy or favour parties at the EU level that they would not want to govern them nationally, for example, parties vocally opposing the European Union. In the 2009 EP election 41 MEPs were elected from 29 parties that were not then represented in the national parliaments of the 17 countries from which they were returned.

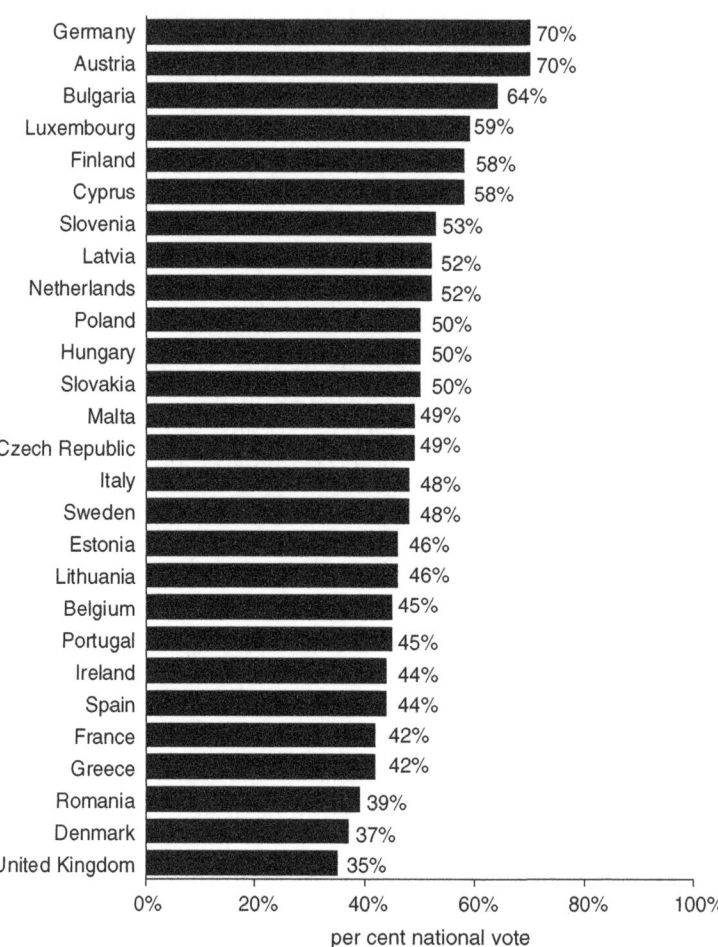

Figure 4.1. Extent national governments represent their electorates

Sources: European Journal of Political Research, Political Data Yearbook 2005, 2006, 2007 and <http://www.parties-and-elections.de>.

Hundreds more MEPs represented parties in opposition to the national governments that represented *(sic)* them in the European Council.

National parliaments have a formal right to receive notice of pending EU legislation and have committees to scrutinize what the EU is doing. However, the volume of EU legislation is such that it is virtually impossible for a small group of national MPs to scrutinize EU legislation in detail. It is not the job for which they are elected nor do they have a staff equal in size to that of the national government's Permanent Representative in Brussels. By contrast with the Parliament before 1979, which was filled by national parliaments rather than election, the EU today gives national parliaments very little right to exert influence over what it does. There is a procedure that requires EU review of a Commission proposal if one-third of national parliaments question it. However, it took two years after the creation of this right for it to be invoked for the first time by a coalition of national parliaments. In practice, few actions of government ministers in Brussels are subject to debate in national parliaments. Even if an EU decision is unpopular nationally, the government can secure a grudging vote of confidence thanks to party loyalty. If a national parliament fails to transpose EU decisions into national laws, the national government can be held to account by the European Commission and the Court of Justice.

British politics demonstrates the difficulties that a national government faces when there are competing pulls at the European and national levels. From the time of Britain's initial application to join the EU in the early 1960s, both major parties have been divided on European issues. The Conservative government of Edward Heath secured parliamentary endorsement of British membership due to a split in the Labour opposition offsetting a split in the Conservative ranks. Although Tony Blair was personally keen for Britain to join the euro, he avoided splitting his government by allowing the Labour Chancellor of the Exchequer, Gordon Brown, to veto Britain joining the Eurozone. The European Union was able to adopt the Lisbon Treaty only because Gordon Brown, by then Prime Minister, had clung to office until spring 2010. Had the Conservatives gained office sooner, there would have been a national referendum on the Treaty. The outcome of a British referendum would almost certainly have been the failure of the Lisbon Treaty to come into effect. The current Conservative prime minister, David Cameron, is subject to conflicting pulls from his pro-EU coalition partner, the Liberal Democrats, and anti-EU backbench Conservative MPs. Moreover, the British government has strengthened national as against European Council pressures by a 2011 Act of Parliament that obligates the government of the day to call a referendum on any future treaty change or transfer of powers from Britain to Brussels.

To avoid the tension arising from competing pulls, national governments have preferred to follow the Monnet strategy of integration by stealth, agreeing policies in the European Council without debate in their national parliament. The conditions for doing so are that the issue is of limited political relevance and visibility, and it is not an object of domestic partisan dispute. While most issues that COREPER considers meet these criteria, controversial issues dominate the political agenda. The Eurozone crisis is a spectacular example of EU politics becoming highly visible, high in impact, and imposing immediate costs. In addition, the treaty on the economic governance of the Eurozone is designed to extend the visible and controversial influence of the

EU by making its institutions a visible partner in the annual debate about national budgets in 25 member states.

II Consultation with Organized Interests

The European Commission describes its proposals as in the common interest of Europe, but such rhetoric refuses to recognize that politics is about recognizing and resolving conflicting views of what the common interest is. There are fundamental political differences about whether the EU's single market should be a social market or a free market. In a free market there is a minimum of state regulation and maximum scope for private choices and private enterprises. It is reflected in the single Europe market's emphasis on repealing national regulations that have been part of the continental tradition of state management of the economy. By contrast, the social market, often described as the European social model, endorses the government distributing the wealth generated by the market more evenly between welfare state expenditure and private consumption. It also endorses the EU regulation of working conditions.

The EU policymaking process institutionalizes extensive horizontal consultations with stakeholders representing conflicting economic and social interests and with experts who represent scientific and technical knowledge independent of national boundaries. Even though national governments appoint the interest group spokespersons and experts who meet in Brussels, if their views are to carry weight in multi-national committees their appointees must form cross-national alliances based on common interests or shared expert knowledge.

Instead of linking Europe's citizens at the bottom level of the pyramidal structure of Europe's political system, interest groups often represent intermediate 'meso-level' organizations whose members are other organizations rather than individual citizens. Groups representing causes such as animal rights or the protection of areas of scenic beauty are virtual representatives, since animals, lakes, and trees cannot authorize or hold to account those who claim to speak for them.

Involving organizations in the Community method of deliberation is good politics for the Commission. The functional concerns of interest groups, which often cut across national boundaries, are a complement to the national constituencies represented in the European Council. Interest groups lobbying in Brussels show commitment to dealing with problems at the European rather than the national level. Those brought into the Brussels network normally have substantial experience of problems on the ground that complement views formed in the high-rise offices of the Commission's Directorates.

Moreover, if Commission officials and stakeholders agree a measure, this puts pressure on the Council and MEPs to endorse what is agreed, especially measures of interest to a small number of affected organizations but of little or no interest to politicians. Even if some stakeholders disagree with a Commission recommendation, they cannot create a furore on the grounds that they were not consulted.

Institutionalizing the representation of interests. The success of the European Union's economic policies depends on decisions made in the market place as well as decisions made in Brussels. Consultation with stakeholders affected by an EU measure can make for better policy, insofar as their knowledge complements that of Commission staff drafting regulations.

The European Economic and Social Committee (EESC) represents organizations that the EU considers social partners, a term reflecting conservative ideas of society being composed of corporate estates and socialist ideas of collective action. Both reject the liberal idea of political institutions representing individuals. National governments appoint members to three separate sectors of the EESC to represent employers, employees, and 'various interests'. The largest countries have 24 members and the median state nominates 12 members. EESC members in each of its sectors tend to have more in common with sector members from other countries than with co-nationals representing different interests. The Committee is annually consulted on hundreds of measures related to the single Europe market and issues advisory opinions suggesting ways in which the details of proposals can be made more acceptable to affected interests.

The employers' group demonstrates the categoric distinction between representing citizens and legal personalities, that is, formally incorporated organizations. EU business associations are aggregates of national associations or represent trans-national firms in an industry, for example, chemical manufacturers, that are affected by EU regulations. The capacity of business associations to make a significant contribution to economic growth is more important than whom they represent. The German-language description of an employer as 'a giver of work' (*Arbeitgeber*) emphasizes that employers and workers share a stake in the European social market.

Trade unions nominally represent individual Europeans. However, for many years the density of unions, that is, the percentage of the labour force that belongs to trade unions, has been falling. Today, less than one-third of the European labour force belongs to a trade union. Even though unions claim to represent individual workers, at the EU level they do so indirectly because most are actually organizations of organizations. The European Trade Union Confederation has 83 national trade union confederations as members plus 12 European-level federations of unions with special trans-national concerns, such as transport workers. In some member states, because of a history of division by social democratic versus Communist politics, private and public sector unions, and religion, trade unions are a category rather than a united body. Moreover, their focus on wages and working conditions of the labour force does not always represent the claims of that half of Europe's adult citizens who are outside the labour force, such as pensioners and homeworkers.

The label of 'various interests' is apt for the EESC's third sector. About half are market oriented, for example, agricultural, small businesses, and professional associations affected by EU regulations. The other half are as varied as the British Stakeholder Forum for Our Common Future, the Polish Students' Parliament, the French Consumer, Housing and Lifestyle Federation, and the Romanian Angel Association. Each can speak for a particular non-governmental organization but by definition none can do so for all of the third sector's various interests.

The Commission convenes more than two hundred committees to scrutinize the details of proposals that it is preparing to present to the Committee of Permanent Representatives and to review the implementation of measures that have already been approved in principle. Committee members are nominees of 27 national ministries involved in their implementation. Committees can include professional and academic experts with scientific or technical knowledge relevant to the subject of proposed EU regulations. More than half of all Commission rules are reviewed by committees that concern such diverse things as animal welfare and energy networks. While comitology committees do not have the hard power to veto decisions, they do have the soft power of making Commission staff take into account practical details of how a policy is to be implemented.

Article 11 of the Treaty for the European Union obligates the Commission to consult with civil society, an abstract and ambiguous concept. This commitment recognizes that while civil society organizations are independent of the state, they have a stake in public policies sufficient to justify being consulted about what the EU does. The Commission does so by involving non-governmental organizations (NGOs) that monitor, comment on, and seek to influence Commission decisions but do not have formal representation within EU institutions. Contact with representatives of interest groups extends the Commission's horizontal network of links. However, accountability is informal or indirect at best.

The number and variety of organizations commenting on a proposal are deemed more important than who or what the organizations represent. The Commission is prepared to listen to organizations without any requirement that they demonstrate their credentials for representing those whose interests they advocate. Accepting policy relevance as a sufficient qualification for participating in a dialogue is particularly important for organizations that claim to represent such broad constituencies as the poor or rare birds, because it avoids the question: Who elected you? While the absence of individual members is a defect in terms of conventional political representation, as long as an interest group has the funds to maintain a Brussels office, its officials can lobby the Commission. In the words of an environmental organization official:

> While ideally it would be good to get people involved, time pressures mean that the most effective use of my time is to get on with advocacy. In the end my role is not to encourage the most participatory governance, but to ensure the best results for the environment.[2]

The Commission has sought to encourage transparency by establishing a register of the characteristics of organizations lobbying it. It enables groups to report information relevant to evaluating their representative status, such as when and where they were founded, whether their members are other organizations or actual people, how they are governed, and where their money comes from. However, to respect the independence of non-governmental organizations, registration is not a condition for participating in meetings with the Commission. To date several thousand groups have registered but some have not done so because of their suspicion that a voluntary register could lead to EU regulation of their activities.

Brussels-based organizations that represent views at the EU level are the Commission's preferred partner for dialogue, because they avoid the need for consultation with 27 national groups. Whatever the nominal interest that a European organization represents, it must maintain an office in Brussels. Because many non-governmental organizations have difficulty in financing a Brussels office, the Commission funds some to write reports and hold conferences on themes that promote European integration. In doing so, the Commission benefits from group readiness to campaign on behalf of consensus recommendations by the Commission and neutralizes potential criticisms. A German assessor has described those receiving Commission funds as 'astroturf' rather than grass-roots organizations.[3]

The Commission welcomes multiple and diverse participants in discussions about its policies as a complement and a potential check on the institutional requirement to engage with MEPs, national officials in COREPER, and the Council of Ministers. Discussions in Brussels or even via the Internet enable the Commission to claim to speak for all stakeholders affected by a policy. It thus provides what the German philosopher Jürgen Habermas calls communicative legitimacy. Insofar as diverse participants tend to disagree, the Commission can use its authority to decide which arguments ought to be incorporated in its proposals and which rejected.

The openness of the Commission to all types of interests increases the number of participants at the peak level of the EU system. The European

Commission regards this as showing that it is bringing its work closer to Europe's citizens. However, at best this is a half truth; it confuses horizontal discussions in Brussels with vertical engagement with EU citizens across the continent. The great mass of organizations making representations in Brussels lack the capacity to connect themselves, and therefore the Commission, with large masses of European citizens. In the words of an academic analyst, 'The good European citizen disappears rapidly behind the benign horizon of civil society bodies.'[4]

III Reaching Below Member States

Governments have a territorial as well as a functional dimension. Before the European Union developed, each state was the unchallenged top tier of its territorial system of government. The EU adds another level on top of that. The Maastricht Treaty endorsed subsidiarity as the principle for deciding which level of government should take responsibility in a given policy area. The term calls attention to the ladder-like connections between levels of government in Europe today, while its vagueness leaves open which rung of the ladder is best for dealing with a problem. Although subsidiarity appears to endorse lower tier action, the EU uses it to justify policies being made through the Community method at the European level.

EU policies are explicitly intended to reach below the level of the state. Spending on economic development targets regions of high unemployment, and agricultural subsidies have a disproportionate effect on rural regions. In allocating EU money, major Directorates of the European Commission deal not only with member states but also with policies affecting regions. It defines three levels of NUTs, the French acronym for Nomenclature of Territorial Units of Statistics, which subdivide member states into more than 1,200 regions. The EU also promotes trans-national policies cutting across national borders or involving multi-national rivers such as the Rhine and the Danube.

Regions. The Commission sees a Europe divided into hundreds of regions as more susceptible to its leadership than a Europe of 27 states. For the same reason, national governments tend to see direct engagement of their regional or local authorities with EU institutions as challenging their monopoly of representing their country in Brussels. For decades national governments resisted giving formal recognition to sub-national governments in the EU system; resistance was strongest from countries threatened by regions seeking independence, such as the United Kingdom and Spain, and also from highly centralized France. The European Parliament has little desire to favour sub-national representation that challenges its claim to represent the peoples and constituencies of Europe.

The *Committee of the Regions* (CoR) was established in 1993 as a gesture counterbalancing the centralizing effect of the broadening and deepening of EU powers. The organizations promoting the Committee, such as German *Laender* and Spanish regions, were overly ambitious in their hopes that it would become a major player in the EU decision process. Its powers are confined to advising in policy areas directly affecting regions and local authorities and to issuing opinions.

The fragmentation of Europe into 95,000 different local and regional authorities means that each of the 344 members of the Committee of the Regions represents a small portion of his or her country. For example, a French member may come from one of 26 regions, 102 departments or 36,678 municipalities. Moreover, even if a member represents a relatively large region, such as Bavaria or Catalonia, he or she is only one voice. Since its members must be either elected or accountable to elected officials in a regional or local government, participating in the Committee of the Regions is a secondary political role. Committee members tend to identify with functional interests that their locality has in common with many areas of the EU, such as agriculture or a declining industry. If an issue is ideological as well as territorial, partisan values become relevant and Committee members are organized into trans-national Party Groups.

Since the Committee of the Regions meets in plenary sessions only five times a year, fulltime Brussels lobbies have more opportunities for influence. Upwards of 250 regional and local authorities have offices in Brussels. They are there to encourage funding from the European Commission and to keep a watchful eye on the Permanent Representative's Office of their national government. However, unless a region or city has political clout domestically, a Permanent Representative will give priority to regional inputs that support the national government's policy. Regions in federal states such as Germany have more political weight, since they have the sanction of votes in the upper chamber of the German Parliament.

National governments have not had their claim to speak for their country as a whole challenged by the Committee of the Regions. After the Lisbon Treaty re-affirmed the singular authority of national governments, the Committee of the Regions prepared a major study of multi-level governance, emphasizing the importance of regional and local authorities in achieving EU goals. Its recommendations have had little impact. It is rhetorical overkill for the Commission to claim that consulting with regional officials 'strengthens democratic legitimacy by working with the people (*sic*) of Europe'.

Reaching down to citizens. As part of its public relations programme, the European Commission conducts semi-annual Eurobarometer surveys of public opinion in all member states. It also conducts ad hoc surveys about policies of special interest to a Directorate or about events to which the

Commission must react quickly. From the Commission's point of view, the Eurobarometer is market research on behalf of its activities. Many questions are designed to help the Commission find out how it can better promote support for its policies from Europe's citizens. For example, a survey can identify whether the lack of support for a policy is due to a lack of knowledge or to specific features that make it unpopular.

Commission Directorates use surveys to demonstrate that there is a popular demand for what they want to do. When the Committee of the Regions was frustrated by the secondary role assigned its members in the Lisbon Treaty, it commissioned a Special Eurobarometer Survey in 2008 that asked if people wanted the regions to have more influence in EU policymaking. In its subsequent recommendations for strengthening the role of regions and local authorities in the EU, the Committee invoked Eurobarometer figures showing that 50 per cent trusted their local and regional elected representatives compared to 34 per cent trusting their national government.[5] However, European polling data is insufficient to budge member states from their positions. The opinion polls that they pay attention to are those that canvass their own electorate.

The Lisbon Treaty has authorized a European Citizens' Initiative that enables citizens to petition the Commission to consider an issue. The rules for the Initiative show the EU's resistance to giving its citizens an effective voice. Petitions are limited to recommendations for policies within the EU's existing powers; the right to alter the EU's powers continues to be reserved exclusively to member states. An Initiative must have valid signatures from a minimum of one million citizens from at least seven EU member states. In an EU setting, to require signatures from only one-fifth of one per cent of citizens is a low threshold. However, given the diversity of member states in the EU, organizing an Initiative requires a great deal of multi-national co-ordination. It requires a publicity campaign in many languages to alert citizens that a petition is being circulated; the capacity to mobilize and train thousands of volunteers to collect valid signatures; and millions of euros to pay for these activities.

To describe the right of citizens to petition the EU as an Initiative is misleading. The normal political science definition of an Initiative is that it triggers a popular vote on a proposal set out in an Initiative petition. This is the practice in Switzerland and in California, where frequent use is made of the Initiative. By contrast, a successful EU Initiative does no more than require a Commission representative to meet with the petition's organizers and make a formal response setting out actions that it intends to take, if any, and its reasons. In effect, the Initiative is a controlled experiment for engaging Europe's citizens in EU affairs; control remains in the hands of the European Commission.

IV Constituting an Ever Closer Union?

The constitution of a state establishes what the government can do, how it can make decisions, and what rights and obligations its citizens have. A majority of EU member states have had to adopt a constitution after their country became a fully fledged democracy. It normally involves a complex process of deliberation and approval by some sort of super-majority. In order to secure popular commitment, the constitutional convention may be elected or a national referendum may be required to endorse the document it prepares. In Sweden a constitutional amendment approved by a vote of the unicameral *Riksdag* is adopted only if it is again approved after a new *Riksdag* is elected.

The EU does not have a constitution; its organic laws are a series of treaties signed by states. The founding Treaty of Rome was enacted in 1957 after being discussed among an elite few, drafted by lawyers, and approved in elite negotiations. The subsequent growth in EU powers has been achieved by additional treaties that augment the founding document. Each new treaty has been prepared by elites. When national governments approve a treaty, their citizens are bound by it. However, from a political perspective treaties signed after intergovernmental conferences in foreign countries can hardly be said to represent the 'will' of the citizens whose governments approved it. The result is that treaties lack the popular commitment that Europeans give to their national constitution.

The deepening and broadening of the EU has increased the impact of EU policies on citizens, and the accumulation of treaties has created a tangle of documents that lack the order and clarity of a constitution enacted at a single point in time. This shortcoming has been of particular concern to continental lawyers, whose outlook differs from that of English lawyers accustomed to dealing with an uncodified and in parts unwritten Constitution. Facing the prospect of adding a dozen states as members, EU leaders sought to revise their institutions in what became the 2001 Nice Treaty. However, the results produced after a great deal of wrangling were deemed inadequate by the governments that signed it.

When the European Council met at Laeken, Belgium in 2001, it had before it a proposal from the Committee of Permanent Representatives in Brussels suggesting that a Convention be called to produce a number of options for reform. In the Laeken Declaration the European Council expressed formal confidence that the EU's role 'admirably matches the wishes of citizens'. However, it admitted that although 'citizens undoubtedly support the Union's broad aims, they do not always see a connection between those goals and the Union's everyday action'. From this, it reasoned that the EU needed to become 'more democratic, more transparent and more efficient' in order 'to bring citizens closer to the European design' of an ever closer Union. To this end the European Council authorized a Convention on the Future of Europe that was charged with deliberating about a constitution for the Union. Whatever the Convention produced would then be reviewed by an Inter-Governmental Conference of heads of national governments that would retain the right to accept, amend, or reject its recommendations.[6]

Although there was a notional intent to bring citizens closer to the Union, none of the members of the Constitutional Convention was elected to sit there. Instead, members were selected from *ex officio* groups. Each national parliament, including the 13 states then candidates for membership, chose two MPs to participate; each national government, including candidate countries, had one representative; and the European Parliament named 16 MEPs. In addition there were two representatives of the Commission and a number of EU staff served as observers or alternates. Representatives of national governments were there to make sure that the draft Constitution was kept within the bounds of what was politically acceptable to them. Although MPs were nationally elected, the national parliaments appointing them were not particularly interested in monitoring what they did there. The 16 MEPs had far greater experience and knowledge of how existing EU institutions did and did not work as well as an interest in strengthening the role of the EU and the Parliament of which they were members.

The equal representation of states in the Convention was consistent with it being an intergovernmental agreement, albeit discussions could not hide the fact that some participants spoke for more important states than others. Having almost two-fifths of participants coming from countries that were not yet members of the EU showed an awareness that the Convention's recommendations were directed at the future. However, it also meant that many Convention members had no experience of how EU institutions actually worked, a characteristic shared by some national MPs.

The European Council sought to promote discussion of Convention issues by establishing a Forum that was 'broadly based and involved all citizens'. The Forum's website categorized the 500-plus non-governmental organizations represented there under the headings: political or public authorities; socio-economic groups; academic institutions and think tanks; and other. The great majority had their offices in Brussels. This is a good credential for understanding how the EU works, but represents a very narrow segment of Europe's citizens. The Forum reflected the EU practice of claiming that the organizations it consulted were equivalent to an assembly with democratic credentials for representing citizens.

The Convention leaders took seriously their call to address the future of Europe by drafting a Constitution for an ever closer Union. There was also a recognition that failure to achieve consensus would result in the European Council dismissing their efforts. Drafting was concentrated in the hands of the chair, the former French President Valéry Giscard d'Estaing, and his staff, and then discussed in a 13-member Presidium. When draft measures were debated in the full Convention, no amendments were permitted. There were no recorded votes, since they would have revealed differences of opinion. Giscard d'Estaing used the power of the chair to allow little time to debate controversial issues and he decided when a consensus had been reached. Only four members signed a minority report calling attention to the absence from the Convention's deliberations of views questioning the desirability of an ever closer Union.

The Constitution included provisions making it easier to introduce Qualified Majority Voting for measures where unanimity had previously been required. There was no *Ruckverlagerunsklause*, that is, a stipulation that powers could be returned to member states. In recognition of the value of the EU having symbols of statehood, the Constitution formally authorized a flag; an anthem, Beethoven's Ode to Joy; and a motto, United in Diversity. The first draft of the preamble contained the statement that the EU was democratic because 'power is in the hands not of a minority but of the whole people'; it was subsequently modified to the more ambiguous phrase, power is in the hands of 'the greatest number of people'.

When heads of national governments considered the Convention's proposals, they resolved issues that the draft had left open and their technical advisers reduced the ambiguities, contradictions, and gaps in the hastily prepared document. The great bulk was unaltered. The preamble statement that power was in the hands of the greatest number of people was dropped. The European Council endorsed the constitutional document as a treaty to be ratified by member states.

5

Referendums—Too Much Participation?

Reforms in the EU are not just a question of aggregating preferences by a predefined procedure. Instead, the procedure itself has to be chosen.

Daniel Finke et al., *Reforming the European Union*

A referendum gives citizens the choice of approving or rejecting a specific policy; this makes it an institution of direct rather than representative democracy. By contrast, elections are broad-brush institutions that only indirectly influence policy. Voters are restricted to choosing the party or candidate with views closest to their own, even at the cost of endorsing some policies inconsistent with their own preferences. There is a risk in inferring that voters who give a party an electoral majority approve of all its policies. A referendum on a single issue avoids this confusion.

A referendum that endorses a government decision enables advocates of representative democracy to claim that such a system is redundant and unnecessary because the government knows what the people want. However, if a proposal is rejected, it demonstrates that the government is less representative of its national citizens than it claims to be in Brussels. Even though most referendums on EU issues are approved, there have been enough defeats to show that national governments do not always represent their citizens at the EU level.

A referendum gives citizens a sanction to enforce accountability. It extends the horizontal checks and balances of EU institutions to the vertical dimension of relations between governors and governed. The monitoring function of referendums is particularly relevant in a European Union context, because otherwise the greatest pressure on national governments in the European Council is to give priority to joining a consensus with governments from other states. The prospect of a referendum can make governors hesitate before agreeing to measures that they realize would be difficult to defend to their own electorate. Even though governors decide whether a referendum is to be held and set the text of the question, voters are the principal actors in deciding whether what their representatives approve will become law. In the words of Liesbet Hooghe and Gary Marks, 'Referendums shift the initiative to citizens and single-issue groups and disarm party elites.'[1]

The Treaty on the European Union declares that 'the Union shall be founded on representative democracy'. The popular election of a parliament is universally accepted as a necessary qualification for a political system being democratic. However, there is no agreement about the need to give citizens a vote in referendums. Theories of representative democracy reject the referendum. The trusteeship doctrine of Edmund Burke holds that representatives ought to take decisions according to their own judgement because their continuing engagement with issues gives them a much better understanding of policies than that of ordinary citizens. Periodic elections are deemed sufficient to hold representatives accountable for how they exercise their judgement. The founders of the European Union saw themselves as trustees of the interests of Europeans. In the words of Jean Monnet, 'I thought it wrong to consult the peoples of Europe about the structure of a Community of which they had no practical experience.'[2]

In a national political system periodic elections give citizens the opportunity to hold governors accountable and eject from office those they see as misrepresenting them. However, this cannot be done at the EU level. A vote for or against a national slate of MEPs cannot change those formulating EU policies, because a country's MEPs are a very small fraction of the European Parliament's membership; national governments making decisions in the Council are elected for different reasons at different times; and the heads of the European Commission are appointed not elected.

Referendums can be endorsed as an addition to the EU's repertoire of institutions imposing checks and balances. The need for EU policymakers to consider popular acceptance of their measures can modify proposals attractive to European elites. Even if the result of a referendum campaign re-affirms the representative claims of governors, this is a small price to pay for clear confirmation that governments represent their citizens. Unlike a Eurobarometer poll in which the median respondent may be a 'don't know' or an inconclusive deliberative forum that lacks binding force, a referendum can produce a binding outcome. Moreover, a referendum victory tends to marginalize critics, since they have had their say and their views have been rejected by a majority of their fellow citizens.

Referendums are endorsed as desirable because they offer the mass of citizens a chance to participate in political decisionmaking. From this perspective, decisions made by a popular vote of citizens have a superior claim to legitimacy than decisions taken by representatives. The justification is particularly relevant for citizens who do not trust EU officeholders who are nominally their trustees (cf. Table 1.1). In response to the argument that most citizens are '*lumpen*' Europeans, with little knowledge or interest in EU affairs, participatory democrats argue that referendum campaigns force elites to inform and educate citizens about European integration and there is empirical evidence that this can be the case.

In practice a referendum combines elements of representative and direct democracy. On the one hand, trustees retain the power to decide whether a referendum will be held. The wording of a referendum question is decided by policymakers. Although the European Council can determine the policy that is put to a vote it cannot determine what voters decide. Nonetheless, the European Council does not have to take No for an answer. When national referendums have rejected an EU treaty, as in Ireland and Denmark, EU policymakers have put pressure on national governments to ask their citizens to vote again and vote Yes. Cosmetic amendments to the treaty have been used to justify and win a re-run referendum.

An EU referendum gives people a say about treaties that determine how they are governed as citizens of Europe. It is not inherently about promoting or preventing European integration. Referendums sometimes endorse and sometimes reject proposals to move toward an ever closer Union. The function of a referendum is to determine whether a majority of voters are for or against a measure. Participation in a vote implies that losers as well as winners are committed to accepting the result, whether they like it or not. Thus, the 48 per cent of Swedes who voted against EU membership in 1994 have accepted that Sweden belongs to the EU and the 48 per cent of Norwegians who voted for EU membership in the same year have accepted their country remaining outside the EU. The absence of a referendum on joining the Eurozone in the 17 countries that did so deprives national leaders of popular justification for the acceptance of Eurozone obligations. In the two countries that did hold referendums about adopting the euro, this is not a problem, because in Denmark and Sweden national majorities voted to keep their national currency.

A plebiscite differs from a referendum because the government of the day not only determines the question but also controls the outcome. For a referendum to be democratic there must be a risk that a government-endorsed measure could be defeated. The rejection of some EU referendum proposals is evidence that ballots are democratic. However, the experience has made EU policymakers shy of risking the rejection of major policies that they produce after lengthy deliberations. Since every free election carries the risk of defeat, the surest way to avoid the risk is not to take any action that could trigger one or another member state calling a referendum. This can be done by confining policymaking to issues that are low in political salience. The alternative is to circumvent the requirement of some member states for a referendum on a treaty by a process of tortuous reasoning that holds that something that looks like a treaty, reads like a treaty, and has the effect of a treaty is not a treaty. This is the strategy that has been followed in the adoption of the 2012 Treaty on Stability, Coordination and Governance in the Economic and Monetary Union.

I Circumventing Europe's Citizens

Decisionmaking by representatives and decisionmaking by referendums are appropriate for different types of policies. Decisionmaking by elected representatives is used everywhere for actions that government can take within the limits of its constitution. This covers the great majority of decisions that governments take. Referendums are appropriate for policies that change the rules by which governments can act, such as the adoption or amendment of a national constitution or the adoption of a European Union treaty.

A proposal to adopt a new EU treaty is comparable to making major changes in a national Constitution, because it confers new powers on EU institutions. Less than half the member states of the European Union have a legal requirement for holding a referendum on constitutional amendments. However, when a change in a country's constitution is proposed almost every system requires approval by a formula that requires a higher level of assent than normal legislative procedures. This may be some form of super-majority, approval by more than 50 per cent of those voting, or a concurring majority in ballots taken by at least two different institutions.

Citizens say No. The EU procedure for adopting the Constitution prepared by a convention of EU representatives was no different from that for treaties. It required unanimous approval by national governments meeting in the European Council and unanimous ratification by member states. The EU requirement of unanimity is more stringent than that for amending the national constitutions of member states. It is also a higher barrier than that required to amend the United Nations Charter, which can be altered if two-thirds of member states, including the five permanent members of the Security Council, approve.

Theories of representative government assume that unanimous endorsement by national representatives in the European Council signifies popular approval. However, a national government's signature is the penultimate, not the final legal step for a treaty to come into effect. In addition, the appropriate institution in each member state must ratify it. Consistent with subsidiarity, each EU member is free to choose the method it prefers to ratify a treaty. In the debate on the EU Constitution, the insistence on national discretion was underscored by national governments rejecting a proposal to hold a pan-European referendum on the Constitution. However, although most member states regarded parliamentary approval as sufficient, nine viewed the Constitution's self-description as the foundation for the future of Europe as justifying a national referendum to confirm the commitment of their citizens. The prime minister of Luxembourg, which had not held a referendum on any previous EU treaty, explained that doing so was appropriate because the Constitution had a 'sovereign dimension'. There were also domestic pressures that made it politically expedient to do so. The British government of Tony Blair pledged a referendum in order to remove Europe as an issue from a pending British general election.

The first countries to approve the Constitution, Hungary and Lithuania, did so by votes in their national parliaments in autumn 2004. When Spain held the first referendum in 2005, 77 per cent of its voters endorsed the Constitution. The next referendums were in France and the Netherlands. Even though both countries had governments firmly committed to an ever closer Union, majorities in both rejected the Constitution. In France 55 per cent were negative; among Dutch voters 62 per cent rejected the Constitution. Even though the outcome was the same in both countries, the campaigns differed. In France there was a long and heated campaign in which fears were raised about European integration threatening France's combination of state management of the economy and provision of generous social welfare benefits to its citizens. In the shorter and less heated Dutch campaign, party loyalties were more important influences. In both countries, supporters of anti-immigrant parties were more likely to vote against the Constitution.

Even though two national referendums and 16 national parliaments approved the Treaty, the need for unanimity meant the Brussels consensus was not confirmed. The shock rejection prompted the president of the European Commission to call for a period of reflection. An EU observer tartly commented, 'And well he might.'

Not taking No for an answer. The rejection of the Constitution in two founder states was a chastening experience for the EU's political leaders. However, they remained committed to enhancing the EU's powers and doing so required a new treaty. Although the Constitution had failed to be adopted, two-thirds of member states had approved it in their national parliaments or in a referendum before the French and Dutch vetoes. Moreover, most countries that were due to hold referendums when the Constitution was abandoned were expected to favour it. The pressures of enlargement, augmented by the desire of some governments to maintain the momentum of an ever closer Union, meant there was a consensus about treating rejection as a setback from which lessons could be learned so that a treaty could be prepared that would get unanimous approval.

The practical challenge facing the EU's leaders was: how to draft a treaty that would be ratified without the risk of multiple referendums? The starting point was the constitution that national leaders had already drafted. Its existence reduced the risk of re-opening debates between national governments that had already been resolved by compromises. The primary changes were to drop clauses that had attracted the most criticism and relabel the document so that it did not appear to be as important as a constitution. To describe this tactic as cosmetic change is to underestimate the importance of symbols in the European Union. The rejected document had been called a constitution in the belief it would not only make the EU more 'state-like' but also encourage popular commitment like that which citizens give to their national constitution.

The recycling of a depoliticized treaty was authorized by the European Council early in 2007. Instead of discussing issues around a table with representatives of 27 national governments, the pro-treaty German presidency consulted bilaterally with national governments about articles or clauses that they wanted revised or removed in order to make it acceptable to their national parliament without a referendum. For example, the Danish government's legal concerns were met by technical changes in the scope and language of these clauses. Tony Blair made the removal of the word Constitution a condition of being able to get out of his pledge to hold a British referendum on an EU constitution. Within six months a revised document was produced that avoided the big bang approach of the Constitutional Convention.

The treaty signed in Lisbon by all member states in December 2007 was called a Reform Treaty. Many symbols that had provided ammunition to opponents, such as a flag and an anthem, were dropped. Instead of repealing existing treaties and re-enacting them in a new document, the Lisbon Treaty simply amended and augmented previous treaties. The chief changes of substance involved provisions for voting in the Council and postponing a reduction in the number of commissioners, both of which had been objected to by many small member states. British concerns were met by protocols recognizing Britain's right to opt out of some EU measures. The problem of minor inconsistencies between the Lisbon Treaty and the French Constitution were removed by amending the French Constitution. The Dutch Council of State decreed that the Lisbon Treaty was substantially different from the Constitution and the Dutch government seized on this to secure parliamentary approval without a referendum. To satisfy Bulgaria, the spelling of the word euro was confirmed in Cyrillic.

Given the Irish court's position on the need for a referendum on an EU treaty, the Irish government did not attempt to avoid a ballot by arguing that the Lisbon Treaty was not a treaty. A lacklustre referendum campaign was dominated by a vocal opposition and the treaty was rejected in a vote in June 2008. Rejection created a crisis in Brussels and an opportunity in Dublin. The Irish government negotiated minor concessions on points that had appeared to boost the No vote. A second Irish referendum was called in October 2009, after the negative effects of the global economic crisis had hit Ireland hard. A more active campaign in favour of the treaty at a time when Ireland was much more dependent on EU funds led to increased turnout and encouraged some who had previously had doubts to swing to the Yes side, and the treaty was approved in the second round. The Polish and Czech presidents, who had previously withheld their signature from their parliaments' ratification of the Treaty, now gave their assent.

II The Reality of Risk: Dozens of EU Referendums

When referendums are called. Although a pan-European referendum has been rejected whenever raised in EU deliberations, the calling of national referendums is outside the EU's control. It is in the hands of national governments accountable to national parliaments and electorates, and the right to do so is protected by the EU doctrine of subsidiarity. Thus, the question confronting EU policymakers is not whether referendums ought to be held but when, where, and in what political circumstances they are called.

In Denmark and Ireland there are constitutional obligations to hold referendums on EU treaties that transfer powers to Brussels, and the Danes have only once managed to circumvent the spirit of their constitution by avoiding a referendum on the Lisbon Treaty. The Irish practice of holding a second referendum to reverse the result of the first referendum is not the only alternative. If the positive results of a second referendum really do reflect the view of the Irish people, then Irish politicians could reduce anxieties and embarrassment in Brussels by campaigning vigorously in favour of the treaty in the first ballot and mobilizing supporters to turn out. This was done in the May 2012 referendum approving the EU's Economic Stability Treaty, which underpinned the money the country was receiving to prevent domestic financial collapse. After an active Yes campaign that confronted Irish voters with stark alternatives, there was no need for a second referendum: 60 per cent voted Yes to the treaty in the first-round ballot.

In Britain the Blair government's readiness to toy with calling EU referendums on the euro and on the Constitution was immediately successful in deflecting political debate. No referendum was needed about joining the euro because the Chancellor of the Exchequer, Gordon Brown, was against doing so. When the Labour government declared that the Lisbon Treaty did not justify calling a referendum as it had pledged to do for the Constitution, the High Court dismissed a claim to force a referendum on the grounds that the prime minister's promises belonged to 'the realm of politics, not of the courts'.[3] The delay of the British general election until May 2010 meant that by the time the Conservatives gained office the Lisbon Treaty had been ratified. However, the effect of these tactical manoeuvres has boomeranged.

In response to backbench Conservative pressure, in 2011 an Act of Parliament was adopted imposing a referendum lock; a popular vote is required on any future EU measure deemed to transfer powers from Britain to the European Union. The language of the Act, and accompanying statements made by its Conservative sponsors, indicates it applies not only to treaties but also to a variety of mechanisms, including 'soft laws' by which the European Commission has expanded its powers in the past. In Britain the political effect is to place a locked gate on the path to an ever closer Union. However, the political effect in Brussels is less clear. If a transfer of power took place by a Qualified Majority Vote rather than being subject to the unanimity rule, Britain would not have a veto. Nonetheless, Britain would be committed by an Act of Parliament to call a national referendum that could reject the transfer of power. This could produce a multi-level constitutional crisis threatening disruption of Britain's already awkward place in the European Union.

Many EU referendums are called by political choice. A national government can invoke the logic of appropriateness to justify asking citizens to give their consent to an important EU measure. A referendum may be called because of domestic political calculations such as a coalition government being unsure whether it has enough votes to secure ratification by its parliament. If the government thinks a referendum on an EU issue will strengthen its electoral support or divide its opposition, this too can lead to a ballot. The media can clamour for a ballot and reinforce its demand with public opinion polls. If referendums are being held in other countries, this strengthens demands for a government to allow its citizens to vote when Europeans elsewhere can. Opponents of European integration usually support referendums because they provide an opportunity to stop moves towards an ever closer Union.

Doubly divided outcomes. Since 1972 a total of 40 national referendums have been held on EU issues in 22 different countries (Table 5.1). In more than two-thirds, a majority has endorsed what their national government had approved. In 19 referendums about joining the European Union, membership has 17 times been endorsed by votes ranging from 52 per cent in Sweden to 92 per cent in Slovakia. Norwegian voters have twice rejected membership agreements negotiated by their national government. Member states have also called referendums on issues such as the adoption of the Single European Act, the euro, and the admission of an applicant country.

The division of the referendum vote challenges the appearance of unanimity given by the European Council decisions. On average, 57 per cent have voted in favour of an EU proposal and 43 per cent against. Unlike Council decisions, which require a super-majority, no such requirement has been applied in an EU referendum. Since referendums that approve a treaty are

Table 5.1. Referendums on European integration, 1972–2012

Year	Country	Type	Turnout %	Yes %
EU membership				
1972	Ireland	R and B	71	83.1
1972	Norway	NR and NB	79	46.5
1972	Denmark	R and B	90	63.3
1975	United Kingdom	NR and NB	64	67.2
1994	Austria	R and B	82	66.6
1994	Finland	NR and NB	70	56.9
1994	Sweden	NR and NB	83	52.3
1994	Norway	NR and NB	89	47.8
2003	Malta	NR and NB	91	53.6
2003	Slovenia	R and B	60	89.6
2003	Hungary	R and B	46	83.7
2003	Lithuania	R and B	63	91.1
2003	Slovakia	R and B	52	92.5
2003	Poland	R and B	59	77.5
2003	Czech Republic	R and B	55	77.3
2003	Estonia	R and B	64	66.8
2003	Latvia	R and B	73	67.0
2003	Romania	R and B	56	89.7
2012	Croatia	R and B	43	66.3
Treaties and Issues				
1972	France, Enlargement	NR and NB	60	68.3
1986	Denmark, Single Market	R and B	75	56.6
1987	Ireland, Single Market	R and B	44	69.9
1989	Italy, Mandate MEPs	NR and NB	85	88.1
1992	Denmark, Maastricht	R and B	83	49.3
1992	Ireland, Maastricht	R and B	57	68.7
1992	France, Maastricht	NR and B	70	51.1
1993	Denmark, Maastricht	NR and NB	87	56.8
1998	Ireland, Amsterdam	R and B	56	61.7
1998	Denmark, Amsterdam	R and B	76	55.1
2000	Denmark, euro	NR and B	88	46.9
2001	Ireland, Nice	R and B	35	46.1
2002	Ireland, Nice	R and B	49	62.9
2003	Sweden, euro	NR and NB	83	42.0
2005	Spain, Constitution	NR and NB	42	76.7
2005	France, Constitution	NR and NB	69	45.3
2005	The Netherlands, Constitution	NR and NB	63	38.2
2005	Luxembourg, Constitution	NR and NB	89	56.5
2008	Ireland, Lisbon	R and B	53	46.6
2009	Ireland, Lisbon	R and B	59	67.1
2012	Ireland, Eurozone pact	R and B	51	60.3

Notes: NR = Not required; R = Required. NB = Non-binding; B = binding.

Source: Adapted and updated from Hobolt (2009:9). Six Swiss referendums on association not included.

not subject to a second ballot, a one-vote margin in favour of an EU measure commits a country to it. The Maastricht Treaty was endorsed by a very slim majority of French voters; 51 per cent were in favour and 49 per cent against. Nor is popular opposition to an ever closer Union a stable commitment. In Denmark the Maastricht Treaty was rejected by 51 per cent of the voters in the first round, but then approved by 57 per cent in a second ballot. Irish referendums have shown a significant fluidity in opinion; in the second-round vote on the Lisbon Treaty the Yes vote went up by 20 percentage points.

When an EU treaty requires the unanimous approval of all member states, a referendum in one country is, in effect, an EU referendum, since defeat in a single state can veto its adoption. Because each member state decides for itself whether to hold a referendum, European citizens are divided into two unequal groups, a small minority who can vote on a treaty and a large majority unable to do so. Since the Single European Act, the representativeness of referendums differs only in the size of the excluded majority (Figure 5.1). In four of the six major expansions of EU powers, between 97 and 99 per cent of EU citizens have had no chance to vote. Holding four national referendums on the European Constitution reduced the size of the excluded majority to 73 per cent.

Proponents of integration accept a situation in which the great majority of Europe's citizens are denied a vote on treaties because this substantially reduces the risk of a halt in progress towards an ever closer Union. Opponents of EU integration are satisfied with the status quo, because if they are successful in securing a referendum in a single country that rejects membership or a treaty, this vetoes their country's commitment to further European integration, whatever its consequences may be for other member states.

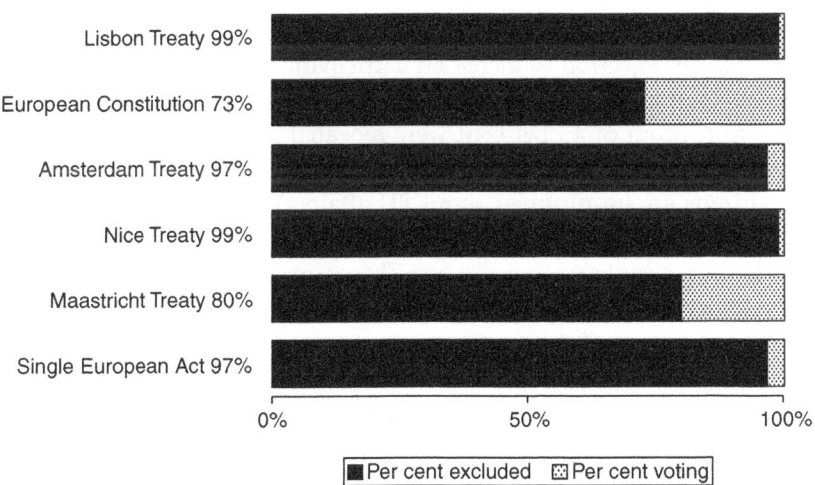

Figure 5.1. Exclusion of Europe's citizens by national referendums

Notes: Lisbon: Ireland voted; 26 countries did not. European Constitution: France, Spain, Luxembourg and Netherlands voted; 21countries did not. Amsterdam: Ireland and Denmark voted; 13 countries did not. Nice: Ireland voted; 14 countries did not. Maastricht: France, Ireland and Denmark voted; 9 countries did not. Single European Act: Denmark and Ireland voted; 10 countries did not.

III Who Wants a Referendum?

Elites don't. In the Lisbon Treaty the EU qualifies its formal commitment to the participation of citizens: decisions shall be taken 'as closely as possible to the citizen'. EU policymakers very narrowly construe the meaning of the word 'possible'. Holding a pan-European referendum supervised by electoral commissions in 27 countries is technically no more difficult than holding a European Cup football competition in a single country. The rejection by EU policymakers of pan-European referendums shows that Brussels will not encourage a procedure that risks rejecting major steps toward an ever closer Union. The proposal for a Citizens' Initiative shows that EU policymakers accept popular consultation only when there are very strict limitations on its effects. Decisionmaking by consensus rejects referendums in principle, since free and fair referendum votes will show that instead of consensus there is a division in public opinion about Europe.

Members of the European Parliament likewise reject referendums as inconsistent with the principle of representative democracy, because they challenge their position as spokespersons for the will of Europe's citizens. This claim is not only a matter of professional pride but also important as a justification for the Parliament's influence on the Council and the European Commission. The EU Profiler survey of party positions at the 2009 European Parliament election[4] found that 45 per cent of MEPs were elected on programmes that explicitly opposed holding referendums and only one-third of party programmes favoured such ballots, with the rest having no opinion.

An empirical objection to increased participation is that people are neither interested in nor informed about European affairs. If the 2009 European Parliament turnout of 43 per cent were repeated in a referendum, a referendum majority would require approval by less than one-quarter of citizens. Many citizens are uninformed about EU affairs. When the Eurobarometer's 2009 pre-election survey asked people whether they felt they knew how the EU works, 56 per cent said they did not. This opens the door to votes being cast in accordance with an individual's satisfaction or dissatisfaction with the current performance of their national government.

There is always the risk of a national referendum producing the wrong (that is, anti-integration) result. To have important EU issues placed at risk by the decision of a minority of uninformed and uninterested electors would, in the words of the President of the European Commission, José Manuel Barroso, 'undermine the Europe we are trying to build by simplifying important and complex subjects'.[5]

Most Europeans do want referendums. Proponents and opponents of European referendums make conflicting assumptions about whether Europe's citizens want a vote on major EU treaties. However, elite debates are hardly evidence of what Europe's citizens think. Nor do they provide evidence of the extent to which public support for an EU referendum comes chiefly from citizens who are against EU integration or from those who are for it.

Immediately following the 2009 European Parliament election, the European Election Study asked: *Should EU treaty changes be decided by referendum?* The phrasing focuses on measures similar to constitutional changes in national political systems. Because the EES question is independent of a specific treaty, respondents are not primed to give an answer that depends on their views about what a particular treaty contains. Proponents of EU integration may endorse referendums as a means of securing popular commitment to increasing the EU's powers. Likewise, opponents can favour treaty referendums in the belief that bringing Europe's citizens into the decision process would halt progress towards an ever closer Union.

A substantial majority of Europeans, 63 per cent, are positive about referendums; this is more than three times the 18 per cent against referendums. Moreover, the 26 per cent strongly in favour of holding referendums on treaties is more than six times the size of those strongly against. The fact that less than one in five are 'don't knows' implies that, whatever is assumed by negotiators of treaties, most citizens are not indifferent to treaties that their national government sign. Moreover, the strong endorsement of referendums is consistent with findings in comparative surveys about national referendums.[6]

Support for referendums extends across the whole of Europe. The chief difference between countries is in the size of the national majority. In Ireland, Greece, and Britain more than 80 per cent endorse a referendum. The size of the majority is more likely to be reduced by an above-average percentage of don't knows than by large-scale opposition. Thus, in Sweden and Slovenia, where endorsement appears least high, pluralities of 45 and 41 per cent respectively still favour a referendum. Support for treaty referendums by an absolute majority in 25 of the Union's 27 countries indicates widespread popular approval for national governments taking co-ordinated action to hold a ballot on the same EU issue on the same day (see Chapter 9). Even if some national governments were hesitant about doing so for domestic political reasons, the example of many countries holding a referendum could exert pressure on them to do so.

Because a survey question is hypothetical, answers may exaggerate demand, while turnout at European referendums provides evidence of the extent to which actions follow words. In referendums held in countries that are members of the European Union, turnout has averaged 66 per cent. Consistent with theories that turnout should be higher at national elections because European ballots are second-order contests, referendum turnout averages 10 percentage points lower than in the immediately preceding national election. However, by comparison with turnout at the immediately preceding

European Parliament election, turnout in EU referendums averages more than 12 percentage points higher than the national vote for MEPs.

The anxieties of the EU's elite about less educated Europeans being more in favour of the referendum are exaggerated. A majority of Europeans of all levels of education endorse referendums on treaty issues. Among those with a university education or its equivalent, 60 per cent favour referendums, and among those with only a primary education, 61 per cent do so. There is also little difference in views between young and old. Among those aged 70 or above, referendums are supported by 60 per cent; among those 25 or younger, 65 per cent are in favour. Because a referendum campaign triggers discussions about the EU that are normally absent in the media, it is a means of informing the politically less interested portion of the electorate about the European Union.

. If people are dissatisfied with the way that democracy is working in their country, they are more likely to endorse referendums as a means of checking decisions taken in foreign countries by distrusted national representatives. The more people see their government as corrupt and performing badly, the readier they are to favour referendums enabling them to challenge decisions that their governors take in Brussels as well as at home.

The biggest cause of anxiety among EU policymakers is ill founded: support for referendums is not confined to the EU's opponents. If that were the case, then only a limited minority would be in favour of such ballots. The referendum demand that the EU elite faces comes from those in favour of the EU as well as from its critics. Among EES respondents positive about the EU, 61 per cent are also in favour of a referendum, only four percentage points less than the percentage endorsing referendums among those against integration.

Treaty referendums not redundant. The logic of representative democracy is that referendums are redundant, because decisionmakers fairly reflect the interests and opinions of their voters. However, the 100 per cent approval by the bloc votes of national governments in the European Council does not match the views of their national citizens. Every referendum shows a divided electorate; those disagreeing with their national government are a substantial minority in a majority of ballots and one-quarter of the time they are in a majority. Citizens at the bottom level of Europe's system of multi-level governance sometimes use referendums to reject rather than confirm what their representatives have done in their name.

Since referendum votes are about treaties that advance European integration, according to democratic theory the division of opinion on integration among policymakers ought to be similar to that of the citizens they represent. Every treaty advancing European integration has the unanimous endorsement of the national governments meeting in the European Council and there is also an overwhelming majority in favour of European integration in the European Parliament. A total of 84 per cent of MEPs are elected on party programmes

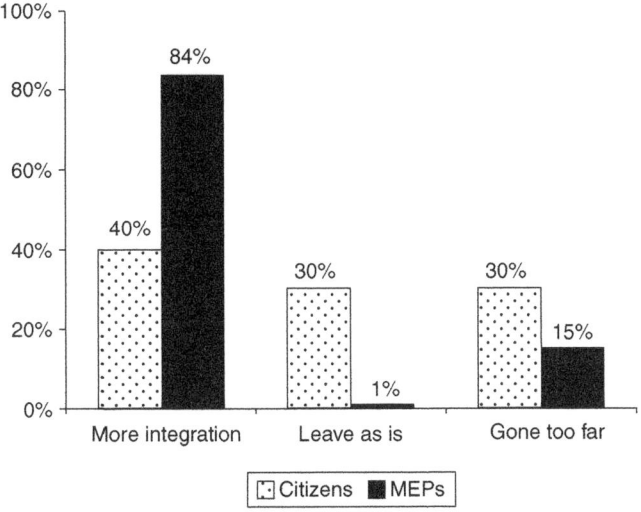

Figure 5.2. MEPs and citizens differ about EU integration

Source: Citizens: European Election Survey, 2009. Number of respondents in 27 countries: 27,069.
MEPs: Data base of policy positions of parties electing MEPs in the 2009 election; see <http://www.
EUprofiler.eu>.

that endorse more integration (Figure 5.2). Support for an ever closer Union
among MEPs is hardly surprising, considering that the way in which they can
have a positive influence is to approve legislation that adds to the cumulative
acquis of the European Union. Likewise, the major Party Groups in the European Parliament have little incentive to articulate the views of anti-EU electors
because doing so would make it harder for them to influence a policymaking
process that was constructed by Jean Monnet to advance European integration
by elite negotiations.

There is a big gap between European citizens and their representatives about
the desirability of an ever closer Union (Figure 5.2). Whereas only 40 per cent of
European citizens favour an ever closer Union, more than twice as many MEPs
have been elected on pro-integration programmes. Thus, MEPs and national
governments do not have an unquestioned popular mandate to approve treaties that irreversibly commit those whom they represent to being governed by
European institutions that they cannot readily hold accountable.

Circumventing direct consultation with Europe's citizens gives EU policymakers the short-term advantage of taking major steps towards an ever greater
Union. Thus, after a few months of deliberation 25 national governments
agreed to the Economic Stability Treaty in March 2012. However, fast-tracking
decisions runs the risk that support for what is agreed in Brussels may unwind
because policymakers have made big and costly decisions without first securing popular commitment at the ballot box through a referendum.

6

Unequal Representation in the European Parliament

In all of its activities the Union shall observe the principle of the equality of its citizens.

Treaty of the European Union, Article 9

The composition of the European Parliament is conceived in such a way that it is not proportional to the size of the population of each Member State. This rather weird situation from the point of view of democracy can be understood if one considers the complex reality of the political system of the Union.

EP Committee on Constitutional Affairs Report, 2007

The European Union is a deviant institution in the world of international organizations, for decisionmaking is shared between a Parliament elected by the popular vote of its citizens and a Council of member states. This gives the EU claims to have a major feature of a state. However, among democratic governments, the European Parliament is deviant because, notwithstanding the nominal commitment to equality of the Treaty of the European Union, it does not represent European citizens equally.

The European Parliament is not elected by the egalitarian formula of one person, one vote, one value. Instead, seats are distributed between member states by a principle labelled by an oxymoron: degressive proportionality. In plain English, it is a system of disproportional representation. The smaller a member state's population, the fewer the number of people each MEP represents and the larger a state's population, the more people are required to elect an MEP. Thus, one Spanish MEP represents 916,000 people, while one MEP from Luxembourg or Malta represents less than a tenth that number.

The mathematical fudge used to assign EP seats to countries is intended to offset the very great population differences between four member states with more than 60 million people each and 11 states with populations of less than

6 million. The resulting inequalities are less than in the heyday of the rotten boroughs in the pre-1832 British Parliament. However, this does not provide a twenty-first century justification. Moreover, it is an unnecessary anachronism, since modern democracies accommodate inequalities in representation by having a bicameral parliament.

Loose analogies with federal systems are often invoked to justify the unequal representation of Europe's citizens. However, the European Parliament is not a bicameral parliament like that of Germany or the United States, in which one chamber represents population equally while the other chamber represents the states that constitute it. Instead, the EP is a unicameral parliament intended to give representation to citizens, but doing so unequally. While many EU countries have a parliament with only one chamber, unlike the EP their MPs are elected in constituencies created on the egalitarian principle of one person, one vote, one value. The European Union is unique in having a unicameral parliament whose MEPs represent very unequal numbers of people. The European Parliament's Committee on Constitutional Affairs aptly describes this as 'rather weird'.

Successive treaties have gradually expanded the power of the European Parliament in the EU's policymaking process. Because control of the Parliament is in the hands of trans-national Party Groups with MEPs representing most member states, the EP can act as an advocate of Europe-wide measures promoting European integration. It can also act as a check on national interests of the Council. Although the EP's powers give voice to elected representatives, it is distorted by the inequality built into the EP's system of disproportional representation. The unequal distribution of votes among Europe's citizens is also a great barrier to expanding the scope of popular election. For example, any proposal to elect a president of Europe is immediately confronted by the dilemma of deciding how to determine the election result. If every citizen's vote were counted equally then the EU's four biggest countries would have an absolute majority of the votes needed to elect a president. If votes were weighted by the EP's existing formula, this would devalue the votes of individual Britons, French, Germans, or Italians by up to 90 per cent.

I From Fig Leaf to Participant in EU Decisionmaking

The governments that founded the European Union did not think it necessary for it to have a popularly elected assembly. It was sufficient for its institutions to be accountable to popularly elected governments of member states. National governments had the exclusive power to decide whether or not to approve measures proposed by the European Commission. For more than two decades after the EU's foundation, a non-elected parliamentary assembly met infrequently and had no effective powers. It was a fig leaf hiding the absence of any effective connection between EU policymakers and Europe's citizens.[1] The introduction of the direct election of the European Parliament in 1979 gave MEPs a claim to represent Europe's citizens, but did little to enhance its powers. It took another three decades for the European Parliament to become a co-decision partner in the making of the great majority of EU policies.

Setting the pattern. The Common Assembly of the European Coal and Steel Community established the template for representing the peoples of the nations of Europe. There was agreement that the supra-national High Authority should give some sort of account of its activities to some sort of representative assembly. There was also agreement that Assembly members should *not* be elected. Instead, 78 members of national parliaments were selected to meet in an Assembly. The Benelux countries opposed allocating places in the Assembly in proportion to national population. The upshot of political bargaining was that Belgium and the Netherlands each received ten seats, Luxembourg had four seats, and 18 seats each were allocated to France, Germany, and Italy.

Smaller states were satisfied with a weak Assembly. They preferred having the High Authority accountable to a Council of Ministers in which each country, regardless of population, had an equal vote. The powers of the Assembly were few and it met for only a limited number of weeks each year. Weakness suited national parliaments. They did not want an Assembly that diminished their prerogative of holding national governments to account. A history of the Assembly concludes, ' "Democracy" was accepted in the form of the Common Assembly, but it should not make a difference.'[2]

The Common Assembly did establish an important principle: instead of sitting as national representatives its members grouped themselves according to trans-national political ideologies. Doing so rejected the Council of Europe practice of members sitting according to the alphabetical order of their surname, as if they had so much in common that neither nationality nor partisanship mattered. Members of the Assembly organized into blocs of Christian Democrats, Socialists, and Liberals. The importance of cross-national ties was affirmed when the first speaker, a Belgian Socialist, Paul-Henri Spaak, was elected by a majority that included German Social Democrats who voted against the candidacy of their fellow German, a Christian Democrat.

The 1957 Treaty of Rome used words almost identical to that of the ECSC when it authorized a European Assembly to represent 'the peoples of the States brought together in the Community'. The advisory and supervisory powers that were conferred by this treaty did not give the Assembly a significant impact on EU policymaking. Its 142 members were a forum for discussing proposals of the Commission. However, the power to make decisions was in the hands of an intergovernmental Council of national governments.

National MPs who volunteered to attend Assembly meetings tended to be enthusiasts for European integration. As elected politicians, they rejected integration by stealth as an appropriate strategy to create an ever closer Union. The Assembly unilaterally changed the organization's name to the European Parliament, a move recognized by the media but not by other EU institutions. Invoking the Treaty of Rome's formal endorsement of a directly elected Parliament, it prepared reports on how direct elections could be introduced. The claim that direct elections would enhance the influence of the EU by giving it popular legitimacy stimulated opposition by national governments hesitant about further integration. The French Prime Minister, Gaullist Michel Debré, favoured technocracy rather than democracy. He 'did not see what direct elections by universal suffrage of a political assembly dealing with technical bodies or with higher civil servants could accomplish'.[3]

The Treaty of Rome authorized the Assembly to draw up a uniform procedure for the direct election of its members, but national governments had to approve when and how elections would be introduced. For two decades there was a struggle between supranationalists who hoped, and intergovernmentalists who feared, that direct elections would strengthen the EP's legitimacy and power. The Council, which represented national governments, was satisfied with the status quo.

The introduction of the direct election of the European Parliament in 1979 was not the result of bottom up popular pressure to democratize; it was the outcome of top-level struggles within the EU system. The Parliament's persistent call to implement the 1957 commitment to direct election gradually overcame the resistance of member states. For the first direct election of the European Parliament in 1979 the allocation of 410 seats to member states reflected the allocation of votes to national governments in the Council of Ministers; the correlation was almost total, 0.99.

Whatever the legitimacy conferred by direct election, the popularly elected European Parliament did not at first have significant influence on what the EU did. With the deepening and broadening of the EU's powers it has evolved into being a partner in taking decisions on most EU measures. When the Single European Act replaced unanimity in the Council with Qualified Majority Voting as the normal procedure for decisionmaking, the EP used this to justify its claim for more powers to check what the Council did. The Maastricht Treaty gave the EP co-decision rights in ten major areas of the single Europe market. It also gave the Parliament power to vote on major EU appointments and to vote no confidence in the Commission. In 2009 the Lisbon Treaty made co-decision by the Council and Parliament the normal procedure for adopting laws and regulations in the great majority of the EU's policy areas.

II Turning Proportional Representation Upside Down

Proportional representation is used in one or another form to give equal representation to electorates in the national parliaments of almost every member state. To secure British acceptance of a directly elected European Parliament, no uniform electoral procedure was initially required. However, before the 1999 EP election the Labour government accepted an EU law that *within* each member state MEPs should be elected by proportional representation. It did so because of the well grounded fear that otherwise in a first-past-the-post election held when the Labour government was unpopular there would have been a massacre of its MEPs. However, proportional representation does not apply *between* member states. Instead, the value of votes depends on national citizenship. Disproportional representation turns upside down the EU's nominal commitment to the equality of citizens. The Constitutional Affairs Committee of the European Parliament explains its use as the result of 'a political fix'.[4]

Degressive proportionality creates substantial inequalities. The Lisbon Treaty defines degressive proportionality as requiring that the ratio between the population of each member state and its number of seats must vary so that each MEP from a more populous state represents more citizens than each MEP from a less populous state. While a degree of inequality exists in the relation of the number of electors to seats in every proportional representation system, the mandating of degressive inequality in the EP is unique among democratically elected unicameral parliaments.

The Lisbon Treaty limits the total number of MEPs to 751. If countries were allocated MEPs in proportion to their population, in an EU of 500 million people, each country would be awarded one MEP for every 665,778 persons. This quota is similar in size to that for the 435 members of the United States House of Representatives, which represents more than 300 million Americans. The ratio of population to MEPs is much lower than in the world's largest democracy, India. In the Lok Sabha, each of its 545 members represents on average more than 2 million persons.

The Lisbon Treaty imposes a floor on the number of MEPs of a member state; each should have a minimum of six MEPs. This avoids Malta and Luxembourg having only one MEP after rounding up their population to make it equal to a single egalitarian quota. It also guarantees five more member states a greater number of seats than they would obtain by the equal application of a population quota. Allocating a minimum of six seats ensures that the national representation of each country in the European Parliament is divided among all the major parties in its national parliament.

There is also a ceiling, 96, on the maximum number of MEPs that a country can have. Without a ceiling, on the basis of population Germany could claim up to 120 MEPs and the four biggest countries would together have a majority of the Parliament's seats. Degressive proportionality prevents this happening. However, the degree of disproportionality is not so great as to eliminate the substantial presence in the European Parliament of MEPs from larger countries. Each of the four largest countries has at least ten times more MEPs than the EU's smallest states and collectively the four biggest states have just over two-fifths of the EP's total seats.

The extent of cross-national inequality can be measured by comparing the population per MEP of a country with that required if national allocations of seats were in accordance with the principle of one person, one vote, one value. An Index score above 100 shows that a country is under-represented in the European Parliament in relation to its population, while an Index below 100 shows over-representation. The EP's rules result in pervasive inequality (Figure 6.1). Only two countries, Romania and the Netherlands, are close to

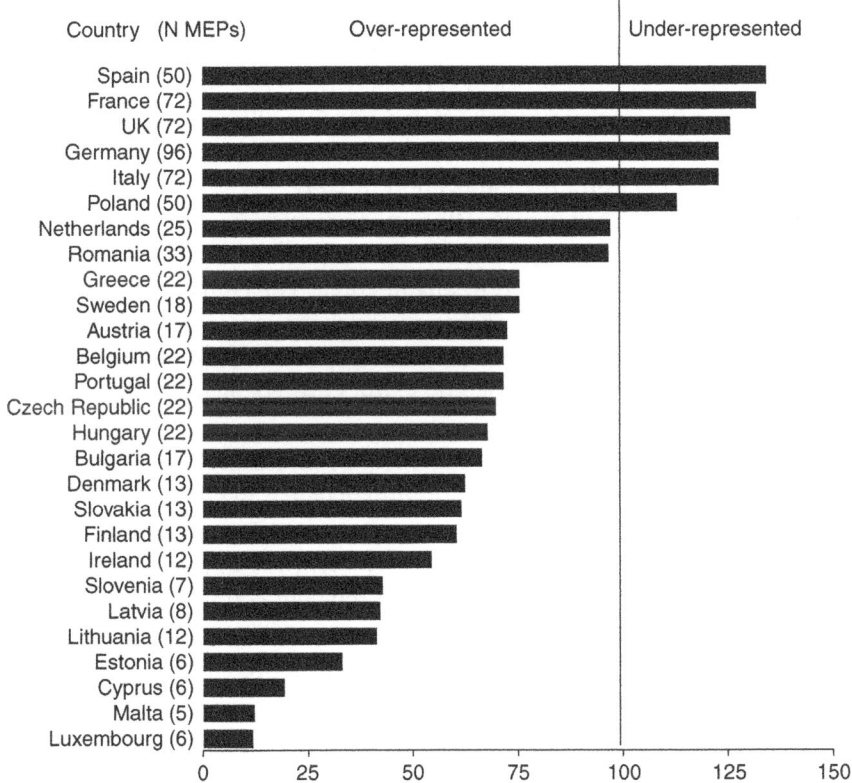

Figure 6.1. Inequality in EP representation, 2009

Source: Calculated by dividing the population per MEP in each country by the population per MEP in the whole EU and multiplying the result by 100.

being represented in keeping with their population. Each of the EU's six most populous states is under-represented. Because the EU has a lot more small countries than big countries, 19 of the 27 member states receive substantially more MEPs than they would be entitled to if seats were distributed equally. Moreover, because degressive proportionality requires that over-representation should increase as a country's population lessens, there are substantial inequalities among over-represented states. What might be called 'larger' small countries have a population quota much less than the pan-European average, but at least half again larger than that of 'smaller' small countries. Malta and Luxembourg have quotas that are one-eighth that of the egalitarian norm.[5]

The over-representation of smaller states reflects path dependence because choices made when the Parliament was created have tended to persist indefinitely. Those who benefit from institutions already in place have strong incentives to use their institutional powers to veto proposals for change. This makes the political cost of revising rules for allocating MEPs greater than putative benefits. There was a correlation of 0.99 between the national allocation of seats among countries in the first directly elected Parliament in 1979 and the allocation in the previous non-elected Parliament. While the number of countries with MEPs has trebled since the EP became directly elected, there remains a positive correlation of 0.97 between the number of seats that the nine EP countries had in 1979 and their allocation in 2009.

Inequality is a matter of degree. The Gini coefficient is a standard statistical measure of the extent of inequality; it is 0 if there is an exactly equal distribution and 1.0 if the distribution is totally unequal. The Gini coefficient for the distribution of EP seats is 0.27, a substantial departure from equality. There is also a substantial measure of inequality among the 21 countries that are over-represented in their allocation of MEPs; the Gini coefficient for this group is 0.24.

Enlargement has had the incidental effect of increasing inequality. Of the 18 countries admitted since 1979, 16 are smaller states that automatically qualify for over-representation. Concurrently, notwithstanding enlargement increasing the Parliament's size from 410 to 751, the number of MEPs of the larger states has been reduced. In 1979 all four big countries had 81 MEPs. Following German re-unification in 1990, its number of MEPs was increased to 99, and the three other big countries had their representation increased to 87 MEPs each. Enlargement has since reduced the number of MEPs of Britain, France, and Italy to 72. The Gini coefficient of inequality has drifted up from a low of 0.19 in 1989 to 0.27 in 2009.

While EU rules can mandate how seats are distributed among national electorates, they cannot mandate which parties people vote for. The partisan strength of each multi-national Party Group is not only a consequence of how many votes its member parties get in their national constituencies but also of how many votes are required to win a seat there. There is no necessary reason for a Party Group's total number of seats to be in proportion to its total number of votes.

Although EP rules require Party Groups to be multi-national, they are not required to be pan-European. Some Party Groups tend to be dominated by parties from big countries (e.g. the European Conservative and Reform Group) or from small countries (e.g. the Greens or the Left-Greens). If the electoral strength of a Group is concentrated in over-represented countries, this will give it a disproportional number of seats in relation to its share of the total EP vote. The bigger the Party Group, the more likely it is that there is a close match between its share of votes and its seats, because it benefits from the large number of seats that big countries have as well as from the over-representation of smaller countries.

Notwithstanding the unco-ordinated allocation of votes and seats across member states, there is a high degree of proportionality between the number of seats of larger Party Groups and their share of the pan-European vote. At the 2009 election the largest group, the European People's Party, took 36.2 per cent of the European vote and 36.0 per cent of EP seats. The difference between votes and seats for the Socialists was only 0.4 per cent and the Liberal Group was within 0.1 per cent of matching its share of the total vote and seats. Since threshold levels and rounding off have more effect on smaller Groups, there is a tendency for proportionality to be a little less there. The Conservative & Reform Group won 16 more seats than it would have been entitled to if seats were distributed in proportion to votes, while the Freedom & Democracy Group received six fewer seats than its share of the European vote.

A half squared circle. A federal system of government combines two complementary principles of representation within a bicameral parliament. It represents individual citizens in one chamber and territorial partners in the other. The EU's requirement that both the European Parliament and the Council must approve policies is sometimes used to describe the EU as having a federal decisionmaking system. However, this ignores the fact that neither institution represents citizens equally. Instead of following the federal principle of balancing inequality in representation in one institution with a high degree of equality in the other, the distribution of votes in the Council reinforces the inequality of representation in the European Parliament. The Gini coefficient for the relation of a state's population to its votes in the Council is 0.35; this is even more unequal than the 0.27 coefficient of the European Parliament. No democratic bicameral parliament has such a degree of inequality in both its chambers.

We can get a sense of whether inequality in representation in the European Parliament is high or low by comparing it with parliaments in federal systems.

The bicameral institutions of the United States Congress and the Federal Republic of Germany are familiar examples of democratic assemblies in which the lower chamber represents citizens, while the upper chamber represents the territorial partners in the federal compact.

The unequal distribution of upper chamber seats to population is at the extreme in the United States Senate. The late eighteenth-century American Constitution treated states equally; each was given two Senators. It was not until the adoption of the seventeenth amendment in 1913 that there was a constitutional requirement that Senators had to be popularly elected. Enormous changes in America's population have today created a difference of 66 to 1 between the population of California and Wyoming. The Senate's Gini coefficient is 0.50, almost double that of the European Parliament.

Qualified inequality is an alternative means of representing federal territories differing substantially in population. Consistent with the principle of territorial representation, members of Germany's *Bundesrat* are not chosen by popular election but by the government of each *land*. The ratio of population between North Rhine-Westphalia and Bremen is 27 to 1. The number of seats assigned to each of the 16 *Laender* varies from three to six representatives. The low ceiling on the representation of larger units results in a Gini coefficient of 0.35, higher than that of the European Parliament but lower than the United States Senate.

The complement of upper chamber inequality is equality of representation in the lower chamber. The American Constitution requires Congress to re-apportion seats in the House of Representatives between states after each decennial census and the United States Supreme Court maintains judicial review of the re-apportionment of House seats in accord with population. The Gini coefficient for the population of single-member electoral districts in the US House of Representatives, 0.04, approaches total equality. It is less than one-tenth that of the American Senate. The German *Bundestag* represents individuals in two complementary ways. Half its members are elected in single-member districts that are expected to approach equality in population; the other half are distributed nationally by proportional representation, which promotes equality of representation. The Gini coefficient for representation in its single-member districts, 0.04, is the same as that for the American House of Representatives. It is also much less than that for the German *Bundesrat* or for the European Parliament.

The German and American examples show that the pursuit of equality in parliamentary representation is not a vain effort. In bicameral parliaments the problem of representing both people and places is squared by balancing the inequality of population in the second chamber with a first chamber elected on the egalitarian basis of one person, one vote, one value. The European Parliament is deviant because it does not balance complementary claims to representation.

III Asymmetrical Representation

Voting is the way in which a majority of citizens participate in politics. There were hopes that the direct election of the European Parliament would stimulate most citizens to participate in EU politics. However, these hopes have not been realized. Even though MEPs represent a more or less indifferent citizenry, they nonetheless have a unique status within the EU system. Whatever the level of population turnout, the European Parliament can justify a claim for a significant role in the EU policy process on the grounds that it is the only institution that represents Europe's citizens directly. The result is asymmetrical representation, because the Parliament has more influence over EU policy than it has support from its nominal electorate.

Most Europeans don't bother to vote. Although the European Parliament does not treat the whole of Europe as a single electorate, it does calculate turnout by doing so. EP turnout figures add the number of votes cast in 27 countries and divide this total by the combined electorates of member states. Doing so gives unequal weight to turnout in different countries. In calculating turnout for the 2009 EP election, Germany, where the national turnout was 43 per cent, is 160 times more important than Luxembourg, where the turnout was 91 per cent. In the 2009 EP contest, 43 per cent of the European electorate voted and 57 per cent did not.

In the past a disappointing level of turnout was explained as a consequence of the European Parliament having few powers; MEPs claimed that if they were given more power they could mobilize more support from Europe's citizens. Since then, the powers of the EU have increased and the EP's influence within the EU system has increased too. However, this has not produced a higher rate of participation by Europe's citizens. In the first election in 1979 turnout was 62 per cent. In the next three quinquennial elections turnout fluctuated between 59 and 57 per cent before falling to 49.5 per cent in 1999 and 45.5 per cent in 2004. Turnout has thus dropped by almost 20 percentage points, notwithstanding the substantial increase in the powers of the EP.

Enlargement has had a depressing effect on turnout. The doubling of the Union's population since direct elections were introduced has boosted the total number of EP voters by 46 million, but the number of non-voters has increased by more than 120 million. In 2004 the whole of the apparent fall in pan-European turnout between 1999 and 2004 was due to enlargement, as citizens in post-Communist member states showed their distrust of new as well as older political institutions. In the new member states turnout was only 40 per cent, whereas in the 15 older EU member states turnout was 49 per cent in both elections. In 2009 turnout in the nine member states that had participated in the first EP election was 47.5 per cent; among the 12 newest member states turnout was 28.5 per cent.

By comparison with first-order national elections, what the EP does is of secondary importance to citizens. EU institutions have virtually no presence within member states. The bulk of EU spending is administered by national officials rather than being disbursed directly from Brussels. Because the ballot is not about who controls government, and the number of seats that a national party can win is far fewer than in their national parliament, parties make limited effort to get out the vote. National parties tend to use the public funds given to them for EP campaigning to meet their continuing administrative expenses and to build up funds to fight their next national election.

Insofar as electors put voting at a national election first and regard EP contests as second-order elections, there ought to be a Euro-gap, that is, a difference between the percentage voting in a country's EP election and in its preceding national election. The second-order character of EU elections is confirmed: in every member state turnout is higher at its national election. The mean Euro-gap is 25 percentage points; for every three electors who vote in a national election only two vote in an EP election. However, the size of the Euro-gap varies greatly between countries. In Belgium there is a difference of only one percentage point in turnout. By contrast, in the Netherlands less than half those who vote in a national election can be bothered to vote in a European election.

Even though an EP election is a common event for all of Europe's citizens, whether people vote is greatly influenced by their national political context. Election turnout differs by as much as 71 percentage points between countries; it was 90 per cent or above in Luxembourg and Belgium while down to 21 per cent in Lithuania and 20 per cent in Slovakia (Figure 6.2). High turnouts in Luxembourg and Belgium have two causes: both countries have laws making voting compulsory and both combine the EP election with an important national ballot. The quality of national governance also affects turnout. After taking a multiplicity of influences into account, EP turnout is significantly lower in countries where government is more affected by corruption and a post-Communist legacy. Moreover, within every national context differences between citizens, for example, in their social class and interest in politics, also influence their likelihood of voting.

Whatever the level of national turnout, in every country there is a high degree of stability from one EP election to the next. The correlation between national turnout at the 2004 and 2009 EP elections was 0.91, and for the 15 countries participating in both the 1999 and 2004 EP elections it was 0.92. Insofar as EP turnout changes within a country, fluctuations tend to be limited and countries move in opposite directions. At the 2009 EP election turnout was up by more than two percentage points in seven countries and down by a similar amount in nine, while altering very little in eleven countries. The stability of national turnout shows the substantial imperviousness of national

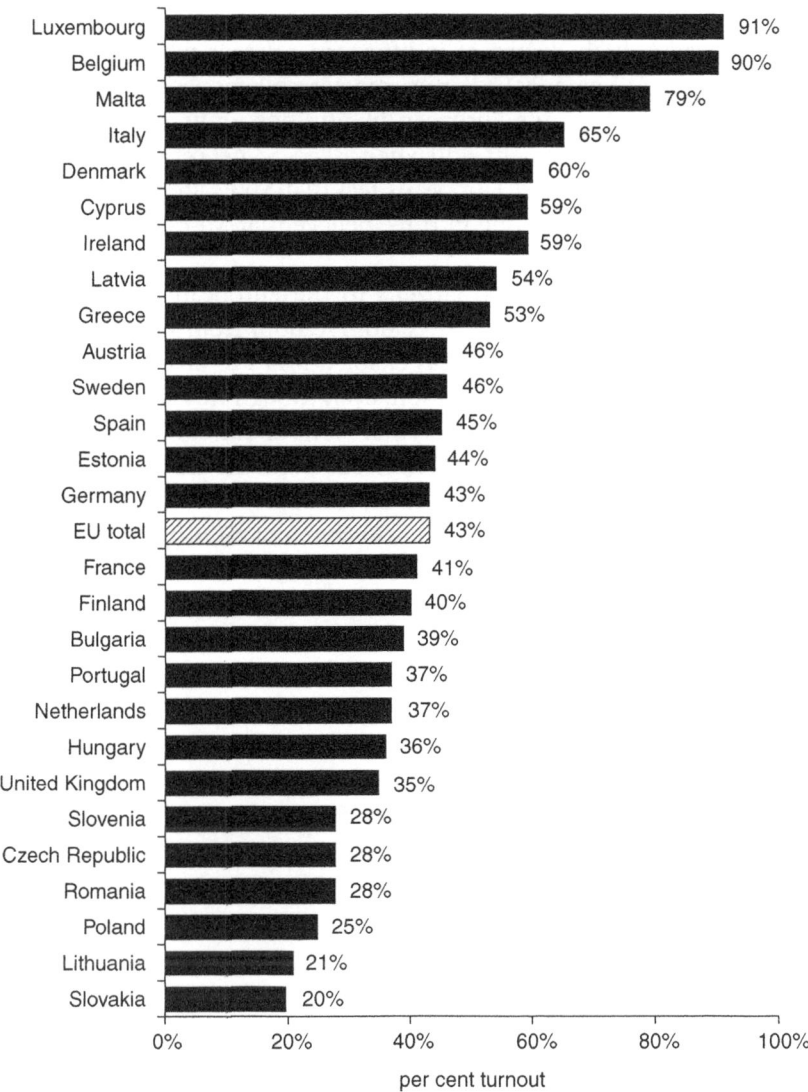

Figure 6.2. National turnout at the 2009 EP election

Source: European Parliament archive, <http://www.europarl.europa.eu/parliament/archive/static Display.do?language=EN&id=211>.

electorates to attempts to boost turnout. In short, the existing level of participation in the European Parliament is not so much a problem that can be solved as a condition that must be accepted.

Low turnout is not an indication of antagonism towards the European Parliament. Public opinion surveys consistently show that more Europeans trust the EP than vote in its election and in a significant number of countries the European Parliament is more trusted than the national Parliament. Low turnout reflects a high degree of indifference towards what the European Parliament does. When a 2012 Eurobarometer poll sponsored by the Parliament asked people to name European institutions, only 53 per cent mentioned the European Parliament, and when asked, 55 per cent knew that MEPs were popularly elected. Most Europeans feel that MEPs are not interested in what they think and barely one in three believe that MEPs do a good job of listening to citizens.

The indifference of European citizens to the European Parliament gives MEPs substantial leeway in what they do. Freedom from the electoral pressures felt in national parliaments has enabled MEPs to give strong and consistent support for European integration, even though this is not the position of many of their voters (Figure 6.3). When views about European integration of those who actually voted in the 2009 election and the parties they voted for are compared, only 48 per cent cast a ballot for a party that matched their own opinion. Of this group, nine-tenths were in favour of more integration. A total of 30 per cent were actively misrepresented, usually because they favoured less integration than the party that they voted for. In addition, 22 per cent were 'over-represented', usually because they did not endorse change in either direction while the party that they voted for wanted more integration.

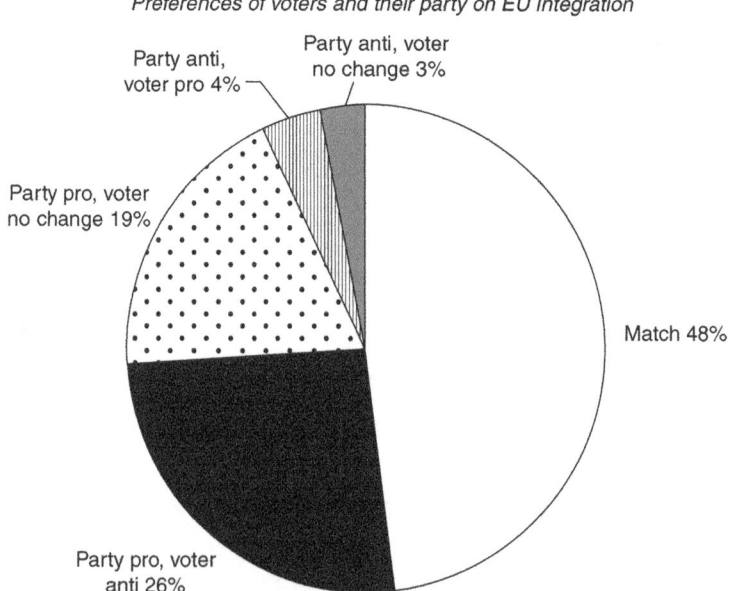

Preferences of voters and their party on EU integration

Party anti, voter pro 4%

Party anti, voter no change 3%

Party pro, voter no change 19%

Match 48%

Party pro, voter anti 26%

Figure 6.3. Most voters don't agree with their party on EU integration

Sources: 2009 European Election Study: all respondents reporting party they voted for. EU Profiler data base of party positions on EU integration.

As long as European voters give priority to economic and social issues and European integration lacks salience, then an inconsistency in the preferences of parties and voters need not cause friction. However, it does constitute a sleeping elephant that could be roused to electoral fury as and when EU actions become both salient and costly. The Eurozone crisis has been a wake up call to voters about the domestic importance of European issues. In troubled Greece, the electorate has gone on a rampage. In the June 2012 election, the party in government when the crisis hit hard, PASOK, had its share of the popular vote plummet from 44 to 12 per cent; the vote for the alternative party of government, New Democracy, also fell. Whereas these two parties, which had alternated control of Greek government for many years, had together won 77 per cent of the vote in 2009, in the June 2012 election their combined vote was only 42 per cent and a majority of Greeks voted against both.

Hardworking representatives of indifferent citizens. Being an MEP is a fulltime job in which three weeks in every month are taken up with meetings of Parliament, EP committees, and Party Groups in Brussels and in Strasbourg. In an average month, the Parliament approves more than 60 laws, regulations, and texts, each of which is meant to be scrutinized. There are additional meetings and travel related to an MEP's particular interests and responsibilities. If treated conscientiously, the workload leaves limited time for an MEP to engage in national politics or to meet the constituents that he or she nominally represents. A survey of Members of the European Parliament found that 83 per cent said working on legislation is important while 40 per cent said representing individual citizens was important.[6]

Multi-member constituencies make it harder for individual MEPs to establish contact with their electors, because the population of their constituency is vast and often its geographical expanse too. In 20 member states the whole country is a single constituency. This means that each of the MEPs from Sweden, the EU's median country in terms of population, has an electorate of 7 million adults scattered over a territory that is more than double the size of the United Kingdom.

The tricks of an MEP's trade are learned by experience. However, at each election there is a high turnover of MEPs. When the Parliament elected in June 2009 first met, a majority of MEPs were newcomers. The high level of turnover has not been affected by enlargement nor does the proportion of inexperienced newcomers alter much with swings in the electoral pendulum in member states.

About one-third of MEPs have previously been national MPs. For politicians from smaller countries or new member states, being in the European Parliament offers a bigger view of the world and often much higher pay than being a national MP. The complexity of the EU's policymaking processes takes time to learn. Only a minority have had the advantage of working in Brussels prior to their election to the Parliament. Since up to 99 per cent of colleagues are unfamiliar faces and often from unfamiliar countries, MEPs need time to build up informal contacts. MPs from countries such as Britain, where single-party dominance is the norm, are challenged by the need to build coalitions across Group as well as national lines. Even MEPs from countries where coalition politics is normal need to learn the complexities of multi-national politics.

The work of the European Parliament involves endless talk among relatively small caucuses of people in committees and Party Groups. While this is also true of national parliaments, the EP is different because its groups are multi-national and multi-lingual. The EP has 23 official languages. If an MEP speaks in the language that he or she would use in their national parliament or when addressing their voters, most of their fellow MEPs would need translation to understand what they were saying, nuances could get lost in translation, and their frame of reference could be foreign to their Brussels audience. Further-more, official translators cannot be used when MEPs of different nationalities engage in the informal discussions that are essential in arriving at a consensus. Over the decades, French and English have been the two most commonly used languages for multi-national conversations. However, these two lan-guages are the official languages of just one-quarter of the EU's population. Thus, more than three-quarters of MEPs must be adept at doing political horse-trading in a foreign language.

With 751 members the European Parliament is too big to accommodate lots of speeches in which MEPs present their views. In each monthly session only half an hour is set aside for individual MEPs to make one-minute statements. Major decisions are made within caucuses of Party Groups and in negotiations among the small minority of MEPs in leadership positions. The organization of the Parliament is in the hands of the Bureau of the President, 14 Vice Presidents, and the Chairs and Vice Chairs of the EP's 20 committees. Within each committee, an MEP who is the *rapporteur* for a significant policy can influence the committee's report, subject to bargaining with other interested parties in the committee.

Each of the EP's Party Groups has members from a minimum of seven states and voting in the Parliament is on Group rather than national lines. Group leaders organize the EP's agenda, distribute its patronage, and negotiate about votes with leaders of other Groups. National delegations can have a spokes-person within a Party Group, but this is meaningful only if a country has a significant number of MEPs. At the bottom of the hierarchy are hundreds of MEPs who have no official post; they include many who have difficulty in exercising influence on others because of being newly elected, limitations of language, personality, or holding views outside the EU mainstream, for example, representing a party that is opposed to an ever closer Union.

Since most MEPs are elected from a party list, their re-election depends on what happens within the national party committee that determines who is listed for winnable seats and who is not. Even if an MEP keeps a favoured position on a party list, the chance of re-election is heavily influenced by their party's standing in national opinion polls at the time that an EP election occurs. This standing is determined more by what the party's national leadership does than by what its MEPs do. Re-election is hardly affected by the performance of multi-national Party Groups in the European Parliament and only in exceptional cases by the performance of an individual MEP. Nor would intensive campaign efforts attract much attention from the media; it tends to treat the EP as foreign news rather than as part of national politics. Electoral incentives that affect MPs nationally have limited relevance in the vast multi-member constituencies from which MEPs are elected. The result is an asymmetry of representation. MEPs spend their time in Brussels in multi-national Party Groups that influence EU policies that affect the lives of their constituents, while most people that they nominally represent appear indifferent to their efforts.

7

European Parties: Integration Before Representation

Political parties at the European level are important as a factor for integration within the Union. They contribute to forming a European awareness and to expressing the will of citizens of the Union.

Treaty of Maastricht

To strengthen the EU's capacity to promote an ever closer Union, the Maastricht Treaty declared that political parties ought to play an active part. Implicit in this was the assumption that European parties could express a common will on behalf of the Union. This assumption is half true: five-sixths of MEPs represent parties whose programmes do endorse an ever closer Union. However, this consensus misrepresents their voters. European citizens do not share a common will about an ever closer Union. In public opinion polls and referendum votes, Europeans reflect three different 'wills': for integration, against, and hesitant or uncertain (Figure 2.2).

The consensus about European integration among MEPs ignores a basic principle of democratic elections: citizens ought to have a choice between parties offering alternative programmes. Within a national political system there are ample institutional means for voters to see what their representatives do in their name and for representatives to learn what their voters are thinking. The prospect of losing votes at the next election is a clear and present reminder to politicians that if they drift too far from the programme on which they were elected, their voters have the power to punish them at the next election.

Within the multi-level EU system of representation, there is a disjunction between the parties that citizens vote for and the parties that take decisions in the European Parliament. The parties that are on the ballot in national constituencies are not the Party Groups that control the European Parliament. Multi-national Party Groups do not contest elections; they are organized within the European Parliament. The most important Groups aggregate MEPs representing more than two dozen national electorates. If an MEP wants to promote interests of national constituents, in order to get the support of a coalition of Groups large enough to form an EP majority she or he must make the case in terms that transcend national interests, such as combatting unemployment or terrorism.

Collectively, Party Groups express the will of Europe's citizens through the policies that the European Parliament enacts. An absolute majority of votes is required to adopt legislation. To be part of a majority, a Party Group must ensure that its members, elected from up to 27 different national constituencies, vote as a disciplined bloc. Since no Group comes anywhere near having a majority of seats in the Parliament, to carry a measure requires the support of several Party Groups. The result is that MEPs who follow their Group's whip often vote together with other MEPs whose party they have competed against when campaigning for their EP seats.

EU policies are not determined by the Parliament; it is one of three partners in policymaking. The initial drafting of the bills on which MEPs vote is done by the Commission. The co-decision process requires endorsement by the Council as well as the Parliament. The process of aggregating the preferences of the supra-national Commission, the national governments represented in the Council, and the multi-national EP Party Groups creates what the Maastricht Treaty describes as 'the will of the citizens of the Union'. It is a will that favours an ever closer Union.

I Aggregation in Multi-National Party Groups

In an EP election each member state is a separate constituency with a party system that institutionalizes divisions according to national circumstances. Parties belonging to the same Group in the European Parliament are free to take different positions when campaigning for votes nationally. There is virtually no co-ordination of campaigning across national boundaries and the rules of the European Parliament forbid its Party Groups spending money to campaign for the election of their MEPs. Each national party determines the programme on which its candidates stand for the European Parliament. In doing so, the party can stress whatever appeals to its national electorate.

Proportional representation requires MEPs to be elected from multi-member constituencies. Because the total number of MEPs is not large, in 21 member states the country as a whole is a single constituency. For example, 25 Dutch MEPs share a constituency that has more than 12,000,000 electors. The division of a big country into regions does not produce small constituencies. The average British regional constituency has almost 4,000,000 electors. Very large electorates make it difficult for MEPs to know whom they represent, above and beyond the national party that gives them a winning position on the list of candidates. While almost all voters will have at least one MEP belonging to a party they voted for, the distance between voters and MEPs is such that voters may not know the name of any MEPs of the party for whom they vote.

Multi-national aggregation. The upshot of the 2009 European Parliament election was the return of MEPs representing 161 different parties from one or another national constituency. The median EU member state is represented by five parties, and five countries return eight or more parties. The median national party elects only two MEPs and almost one-third elect only a single member. Thus, the great majority of parties are far too small to influence an assembly of up to 751 MEPs; they must combine with MEPs from other countries. Their constituents are unclear about how this is done. Twenty per cent of Eurobarometer respondents do not claim any knowledge of how their MEPs ally themselves in the European Parliament and 38 per cent think that the MEPs they elect sit as a bloc that represents their country. Barely two-fifths know that their MEPs sit in multi-national Party Groups.

Because the number of national parties is far too large to organize the activities of the Parliament, its rules require that nationally elected MEPs join trans-national Party Groups with at least 25 members from at least seven member states. While MEPs represent a national electorate, their Party Group aggregates the programmes of dozens of national parties. There are strong organizational incentives for MEPs to join a Group, since Groups allocate resources such as office space and assignments to EP committees. MEPs depend on their trans-national Party Group for guidance about what position to take when an issue comes up about which they have little know-ledge and no political stake. Whatever the national party affiliation of MEPs, their EP votes usually follow instructions from the whips of their Party Group. Providing cues to uninformed and inexperienced MEPs is particularly relevant because of the high turnover of MEPs from one Parliament to the next.

Following the 2009 EP election there were eight Party Groups, including one that is a collection of otherwise non-aligned MEPs (Table 7.1). There are substantial differences between Groups in the number of MEPs and national parties that join. The median Group has parties coming from 14 states. Only the two biggest Groups—the European Socialists and the European People's Party—include parties from all or almost all member states. Since EP rules allow a Group to have more than one party from a single state, the European People's Party (EPP) has 41 parties. The bigger the Party Group, the more difficult it is for MEPs from any one country, even Germany, to dominate it. The price of a national party being large enough to have a dominant influence in a Group is that the Group is not so big that it has a lot of influence in the

Table 7.1. Composition of EP Party Groups

Party Groups	MEPs	Countries	Parties	Votes	Seats
	N	N	N	%	%
European People's	265	26	41	32.0	36.0
Socialists	184	27	28	22.3	25.0
ALDE: Liberals	84	19	29	9.8	11.4
Greens	55	14	19	7.5	7.5
Left-Nordic Green	35	13	15	3.8	4.8
Conservative & Reform	54	8	9	4.8	7.3
Freedom & Democracy	32	9	9	4.5	4.3
Non-aligned	27	9	11	3.6	3.7
Total	736	27	161	88.4	100

Source: European Parliament, DG Communication, Public Opinion Review: European Elections 1979–2009, Public Opinion Monitoring Unit, p. 14, 2009.

Parliament as a whole. For example, the British Conservatives constitute almost half the MEPs in the European Conservative & Reform Group and the Poles more than a quarter, but their Group is of little political consequence because in total it has only 54 MEPs.

In their activities MEPs are much less subject to national electoral pressures than are MPs in a national parliament. Their voters are primarily motivated by national political considerations rather than by what their representatives do in the European Parliament. MEPs cannot engage in a perpetual campaign for votes because they are out of their country for most of the week and their activities abroad receive little or no national media coverage. Party Groups cannot ask voters to choose between different leaders, since a Group's leader will only belong to one of the many countries electing its MEPs. Nor can Party Groups campaign on their record as Europe's governors. Hence, Group leaders give priority to the caucus politics of the European Parliament rather than constantly campaigning for popular support as national party leaders do.

Weak links between Party Groups and European citizens give MEPs more time and incentive to concentrate on policymaking. Much of this work is done in committees that review legislative proposals made by the European Commission. Each committee consists of MEPs from all the Party Groups. Since no Group has a majority in a committee, negotiations across Group and national lines are required before a Committee report can aggregate views of its members into a bill to be presented for the approval of Parliament as a whole.

Party Groups are caucus parties giving intense albeit introverted attention to the activities of the EP and related EU institutions. Each Group has a formal, hierarchical structure. The volume and complexity of decisions facing Groups give leaders significant discretion. Whereas in national parliaments all those participating in such negotiations are accountable to the same national electorate, the leaders of each EP Party Group are accountable only to their multi-national caucus. Since approval requires an absolute majority, Group leaders whose MEPs have competed with each other in their national constituencies negotiate an agreement that overrides any differences. Most EP measures are endorsed without a recorded vote. This makes it easier for a Group to avoid publicly showing internal disagreements among its MEPs.

II Differentiating Party Policies

In competing for seats in the European Parliament national parties differentiate themselves from each other by their policies, since their Group leader is unlikely to speak the language of the party's voters and they are not part of a government or opposition bloc. Among the many efforts of political scientists to identify *which* policy dimensions differentiate parties, the EU Profiler project of the European University Institute, Florence is especially relevant here. Before the 2009 European Parliament election it used the Internet to ask hundreds of national parties to state their positions on more than two dozen policies and to document their replies with statements made to their 27 national electorates (see <http://www.euprofiler.eu>). To avoid being taken in by misleading replies, the multi-national Profiler team independently checked the statements of each party against their public statements in their national language. Differences were usually matters of degree, for example, between completely endorsing and tending to endorse a position.

Given the diversity of countries and parties in the European Parliament, it is unreasonable to expect all parties to fit neatly along a single left versus right dimension. Factor analysis can identify statistically the links between the positions that parties take on specific policies. For example, a party that takes a permissive attitude towards same-sex marriages may well tend to favour legalizing soft drugs, while a party against one of these policies will also tend to be against the other. Five different dimensions of issues are thus identified.[1]

> *European integration* is the most important of all the dimensions characterizing parties. However, the distribution of MEPs for and against further integration is lopsided. Instead of competing, there is a consensus; five-sixths of MEPs are elected on programmes favouring an ever closer Union; only one in six favours less integration (cf. Figure 5.2).

> *Socio-economic welfare* tends to divide the European Parliament almost equally: 48 per cent of MEPs favour government policies promoting social welfare as against 41 per cent showing more confidence in the market. This dimension covers issues such as maintaining social programmes even if it means higher taxes, giving

priority to reduced spending in order to lower taxes, promoting private health care, and reducing regulations about workers' rights in the expectation of lowering unemployment.

Immigration is an integral part of the single European market and immigrants now come from well beyond the boundaries of EU member states. Party positions on this issue are independent of their views on welfare. In all, 43 per cent of MEPs are elected on national party programmes that emphasize restricting immigration and that immigrants should accept the national culture and values of their host country, as against 48 per cent being prepared to endorse immigration and the cultural diversity that comes with it.

*Traditionally, European states with strong religious parties regulated individual morality; today *permissive* issues continue to differentiate parties independently of their views on economic welfare and immigration. Parties that endorse the role of religion in politics are also less permissive about policies concerning sex and crime. A narrow majority of MEPs, 54 per cent, oppose permissive measures while 41 per cent represent parties that accept individual choice in matters of morality.

*Since the EU was founded to protect smokestack industries, *green* issues have become politically prominent. Because polluted air does not recognize any national boundaries, environmental issues are inherently trans-national. A total of 54 per cent of MEPs support environmental protection by promoting renewable energy and combatting global warming even if doing so imposes economic costs. Since a fifth of MEPs belong to parties with no clear position on green issues, only one-quarter give economic considerations priority over the environment.

Consistent with theories of party competition, MEPs are sharply divided on four of the above five dimensions. There is only a three percentage point difference between those in favour and those against social welfare policies, a five point difference in favouring green policies, and a nine point difference in views about same-sex marriages. Immigration shows substantial differences in the electorate: 74 per cent of EU citizens think immigrants should adapt to their host culture as compared to 60 per cent of MEPs.[2]

III What Party Groups Represent

National political parties can seek votes on the grounds that they represent attractive leaders or by having familiar images with which individuals identify. However, the leaders of EP Party Groups are not well known European political personalities. European football players or Eurovision song contestants have more public recognition than the leader of the biggest EP party, Wilfried Martens of the European People's Party, or Johannes Swoboda of the Socialist Group. Party Groups lack images or brand names as familiar as that of Nescafe or McDonald's. Moreover, if people do have a party identification, it is with a national party rather than an EP Party Group.

Party Groups do not have programmes endorsed by Europe's voters. Aggregating the national programmes of the parties that belong to a Group creates the nearest equivalent of a Group programme. However, whether this constitutes a mandate for action depends upon whether the result is coherent, that is, the extent to which the parties belonging to a Group take the same position in the national programmes that they have been elected to represent. If so, a Group is cohesive rather than internally divided.

Political ideologies provide principles that can give policy coherence to a Party Group because they are relevant to policy choices across the whole of Europe. Insofar as parties in different countries share the same ideological principles, then their programmes should be similar. In this way, MEPs who do not appear on the same ballot or speak the same language can find themselves having positions in common on the above policy dimensions. Ideologies vary in their breadth and flexibility. The broader the scope of an ideology, for example, socialism, the readier MEPs sharing it are likely to be in agreement on multiple policies. By contrast, a Group formed around a single issue, whether for European integration or environmental protection, may find its MEPs represent conflicting positions on other dimensions.

The European Parliament does not require a Party Group to have an ideology. Its Rules of Procedure simply state: 'Members *may* form themselves into Groups according to their political affinities' (italics added). The opportunistic pursuit of institutional benefits can be a sufficient motive for MEPs to join a Party Group having an anodyne label that avoids association with any particular ideology. When competing for EP seats, opportunistic parties can tailor their appeals to their specific national context or make a vague catchall appeal, endorsing, like Tony Blair, what works. However, parties that try to appeal to everybody may not win anybody's vote.

The extent to which a multi-national Party Group represents a coherent programme can be measured by an Index of Representation. For each policy dimension it is created by subtracting from the majority position of its MEPs the percentage of its MEPs in the minority. The Index ranges from 100, if the national programmes of all its MEPs take the same position, to 0, total disagreement, if 50 per cent take one position and 50 per cent take the opposite. The higher the value of the Index, the more coherent are the policies that a Group represents. As the value of the Index falls, the more divided a Group is and, if the Group's whips produce unity in an EP vote, a substantial minority will be misrepresenting their voters.

There is very substantial variation between Groups in the extent to which their MEPs agree about policies. The range in the Index of Representation is from 3, almost complete division within the EPP on the green dimension, to 100,

Table 7.2. Policy coherence of EP Party Groups

	EU	Welfare	Permissive	Green	Anti-immg	Mean
	\multicolumn{6}{c}{*Index of Representation*}
	\multicolumn{6}{c}{*Range: Completely united, 100; Completely divided, 0*}
Green	78	94	90	90	−90	88
Left-Green	−37	97	100	94	−82	82
Socialist	100	90	51	83	−73	79
Free & Dem	−78	−45	−59	−68	88	68
Non-aligned	−65	43	−83	−40	100	66
EPP	98	−55	−95	3	52	61
ALDE	100	−14	23	17	−9	33
Cons & Ref	−28	−32	−6	−4	57	25

Minus signs show most of a Group's MEPs are negative.
Source: EU Profiler data as reported in G. Borz and R. Rose, *Mapping Parties across Europe with EU Profiler Data* (CSPP *Studies in Public Policy* 470, 2010).

complete agreement on European integration among Socialist and ALDE MEPs, among Non-aligned MEPs in being anti-immigrant, and Left-Greens in favouring permissiveness (Table 7.2). On each dimension, at least one Group has a very high degree of cohesion, with an Index score above 90.

European Groups historically linked with broad ideologies vary greatly in the extent to which they are united on policy across all five dimensions. Even though some members of the Socialist International have espoused third-way programmes while others are offshoots of former East European Communist parties, the Socialist Group is highly representative of its 27 member parties across four dimensions. Its Index of Representation is 100 on European integration, 90 on socio-economic welfare, 83 on green issues, and 73 in rejecting anti-immigrant policies. Permissiveness is the only dimension with substantial disagreement among Socialist MEPs.

The founding states of the European Union had major parties reflecting universal Catholic beliefs and there was a Christian Democratic Group in the non-elected European Parliament. However, religious parties have waned in strength or disappeared in countries where church attendance is no longer the norm. EU expansion has also brought in many countries from Northern Europe that rejected Catholicism in the Reformation and East European countries where secularism is strong and historic churches do not look to Rome for leadership. Consistent with a catchall strategy making it the largest Group in the European Parliament, the European People's Party has attracted two member parties from most member states. Notwithstanding such diversity, its MEPs agree on two major ideological dimensions: the rejection of permissive policies and the endorsement of European integration. EPP members show substantial divisions on economic welfare, reflecting social market tendencies within Catholicism as against the acceptance of market choice in liberal philosophies. There are also divisions about the environment and about immigration.

Liberalism is a European political tradition with strong nineteenth-century roots. However, in post-1945 Europe there has been no agreement between or within countries about what a Liberal ideology is. Liberal politicians have been inclusive rather than clear in interpreting liberal principles. This is reflected in the compound name of the Alliance of Liberals and Democrats for Europe, which was formed by amalgamating two equally cumbersome and vaguely named Groups. In more than half the countries in which it has members, the elastically named ALDE Group accepts two national parties as members. It is the paradigm example of a single-issue Group; its Index of Representation is 100 per cent on European integration while lacking cohesiveness on all other dimensions (Table 7.2).

The environment is a collective good affecting all Europeans; this implies that Green parties could have an appeal that emphasizes this issue to the exclusion of others. However, the Greens in the European Parliament are not single-issue parties. Instead, their programmes are more left than the Socialist Group. The Green Party Group is the only one in the European Parliament whose members register a very high level of agreement on all five policy dimensions; its mean Index of Representation score is 88. The European United Left/Nordic Green Left Group, which originated as a refuge for former Communists after the fall of the Berlin Wall, is almost equally cohesive across dimensions. If disagreements about European integration are discounted, the Left-Greens are even more in agreement than the Green Group. However, comprehensive ideologies have a political cost. Together, the two left-wing environmentalist Groups have less than half the number of Socialist MEPs (Table 7.1).

The members of the Freedom and Democracy Group represent a nationalist ideology. They agree in interpreting freedom as national freedom from European integration and their idea of democracy rejects immigration because it promotes multi-culturalism.

From its name the Non-aligned Group appears to be a catchall combination of national parties formed for the pragmatic reason of securing EP institutional benefits. Notwithstanding this, it represents coherent policies on two dimensions: its parties are anti-immigrant and anti-permissive society. The racist and often homophobic position of its members, such as the British National Party and the French National Front, suggest that non-alignment is not so much a residual category as it is a cover for pariah parties that are unwelcome on policy grounds by the other seven EP Groups.

The Conservative and Reform Group is the paradigm example of a pragmatic catchall Group without any pretence of shared principles. Its MEPs do not agree about what they represent collectively on any of the five dimensions. It was formed after the 2009 EP election to secure Group benefits for national parties out of step with other Groups. Its leading parties, the British Conservatives and the Polish Law & Justice Party, are on opposite sides on all five policy dimensions, including attitudes towards European integration.

Collectively, ideology tends to join parties divided by nationality. On each dimension differentiating parties, a big majority of MEPs find that there is agreement between their national programme and the dominant position of their multi-national Party Group. Thus, differences between Groups are complemented by a high degree of agreement within each Group. For example, whether they are for or against welfare policies, more than five-sixths of MEPs belong to Party Groups with the same position as their national programme. Agreement is equally high on both sides of the debate about permissive policies.

IV Consensus Supplants Representation

If parties are to be effective in representing their voters, they must have their policies enacted into law. Otherwise, their supporters have representation without legislation. European Parliament approval of most measures requires an absolute majority. Since no Group has a majority, several must combine their votes if the Parliament is to approve a policy. In an adversary legislature such as the British House of Commons, the Opposition sees its immediate priority as blocking the enactment of policies and then winning a majority so that it can enact its own programme. The politics of the European Parliament is very different. There is no alternation between government and opposition parties. Furthermore, MEPs do not have the power to prepare legislation; that is in the hands of the European Commission. Thus, the rejection of a Commission proposal means that nothing is done.

Most MEPs are legislative activists: they want to see the European Union have an impact on European societies. When a sample of MEPs was asked whether they thought there should be more or less EU-wide regulation in seven different social and economic areas such as working time, environmental protection, and food safety, an average of 64 per cent favoured more EU regulation, more than five times the number wanting less regulation. MEPs were similarly activist when asked about extending EU policies in such areas as home affairs and foreign policy as well as trans-national crime and asylum seekers. A total of 65 per cent favoured more EU action, more than four times those wanting the EU to do less.[3]

To avoid the European Parliament becoming a do nothing Parliament, EP committees amend Commission proposals to make them more acceptable to elected politicians and Party Group leaders negotiate further amendments to make policies sufficiently attractive to secure a majority from MEPs belonging to different Groups.

Since no Party Group comes close to having an EP majority, approval of a measure requires MEPs who have competed with each other in their national constituencies to vote together. There are three ways in which a majority coalition can come about. First of all, Groups that are close to each other in the programme commitments of their MEPs can combine in support of what is common in their party programmes. A second alternative is the formation of a minimum winning coalition, so that the political advantages of determining the adoption of a measure do not have to be widely shared among a large and potentially awkward number of partners. Thirdly, in order to secure collective benefits Groups can form a cartel in which Party Groups co-operate to pursue the common institutional good of maximizing the EP's influence in ways meeting the Maastricht Treaty's exhortation to promote European integration.

The political arithmetic of adopting policies. When there are only three positions on a policy—for, against, or neutral—then some Party Groups will find that their position is also held by at least one other Party Group. On three policy dimensions—economic welfare, permissiveness, and European integration—four Party Groups are positive and four Groups are negative. On environmental issues and immigration, four Party Groups are on one side, three on the other side, and one Group is neutral. However, whether a combination of three or four Groups has an EP majority depends on how many MEPs they can muster.

The three left Party Groups have the highest degree of programmatic agreement. For them to combine together creates no internal conflict because the great majority are elected on national programmes that take the same positions (see Table 7.2). However, even if all their votes are pooled, the three Groups do not have an EP majority. The Greens and Left-Greens together have less than one-quarter of the MEPs required for a EP majority. Adding the Socialist Group brings the total to 273 MEPs, still far short of an EP majority.

The non-left Groups have a majority of MEPs, but they are a category rather than a cohesive voting bloc. Collectively, non-left parties are defined by what they are not. The European People's Party, the Alliance of Liberals and Democrats for Europe, and the Conservative and Reform Group together have an arithmetic majority, but there is no policy dimension on which all three Groups agree. Moreover, the third largest EP Group, ALDE, is an awkward coalition partner, because on most policy dimensions its MEPs tend to be divided in their programme commitments.

Since EP decisions are not votes of confidence in government, there is no need for Groups to form a stable coalition. Instead, policies can be endorsed by what the Danes call a 'jumping majority', that is, ad hoc combinations formed on an issue-by-issue basis as MEPs allied on one measure form different alliances on another. By a process that Italian politicians call *combinazione*, ideological differences can be compromised by bargains between Group leaders. The potential for doing so is facilitated by the median MEP on three major policy dimensions—economic welfare, immigration, and permissiveness—being in a party that is neutral rather than committed. Being neutral makes it easier for a Group to bargain for support and the remoteness of the Parliament from European citizens gives MEPs considerable leeway in deciding their positions.

Political arithmetic suggests that a grand coalition between the European People's Party and the Socialists would provide a stable minimum winning coalition for EP legislation, since together they have three-fifths of the EP's seats. However, political ideology appears to be an obstacle to a 'black-red' coalition. Substantial majorities in the People's Party and the Socialist Group take opposing positions on most dimensions. Whereas 90 per cent of Socialists endorse state action to promote economic welfare, 70 per cent of EPP members oppose doing so. When permissive issues arise, 74 per cent of Socialist MEPs give their support, whereas 96 per cent of EPP members take socially conservative positions. There is a similar gap between the two Groups on immigration and on green issues. European integration is the only dimension on which both Groups agree: 100 per cent of Socialist MEPs and 98 per cent of EPP MEPs are elected on programmes that support European integration.

When the European Parliament considers policies, active promotion of EU legislation trumps ideological opposition. Notwithstanding consistent opposition on policies, when roll-call votes are taken in the Parliament there is normally black-red agreement. In 69 per cent of cases between the June 2009 EP election and January 2012, a majority of EPP and Socialist MEPs voted together. This pattern has persisted since the collapse of Communism deprived Socialist MEPs of the option of collaborating with Communist MEPs. In a majority of cases, the Liberal ALDE Group adds its support too. Moreover, the pattern of the Big Three Groups standing together on policy has tended to persist from one Parliament to the next. Some smaller Groups often join, creating an overwhelming majority.

Consensus or cartel? Agreement between the two largest Party Groups in the European Parliament can be justified as a necessary condition for enacting public policies. However, whether a black-red coalition is justifiable in terms of representative democracy depends on the extent to which the policies jointly endorsed by the two EP Groups are consistent with the positions their MEPs have taken in the programmes that they put to their national electorates. If a consensus reflects agreement between the two levels, this is evidence that representative government can work in the multi-level EU system. However, if the consensus is created by many MEPs endorsing policies opposed to their national programmes, this is what Italians call *trasformismo*, a process in which politicians say one thing when campaigning for office and once elected, take a very different position. Insofar as this is the case, when black and red MEPs follow the instructions of their whips, the result is a cartel that deprives voters of having competing policies that they endorse fully represented in EP decisionmaking.

The Profiler data base shows that the collaboration of the two biggest EP Groups to enact laws has a high price: it is more consistent with cartel politics than with representative democracy. The collective benefit that the EP gains by creating majorities without regard to party programmes greatly reduces the extent to which the votes of MEPs match the positions they endorse nationally. Because the European People's Party has a lot more MEPs than the Socialist Group, this ought to give it more weight when making agreements. However, because the Socialist Group is more united on policy issues (Table 7.2), when they combine this gives the Socialists more weight in determining the dominant position.

Even though more than two-thirds of EPP members were elected on programmes opposing socio-economic welfare policies, when they combine with Socialists, there is a majority in favour of welfare policies. Thus, almost half of their MEPs are expected to vote against the welfare policies that they put forward to their national electorates (Figure 7.1). On policies towards

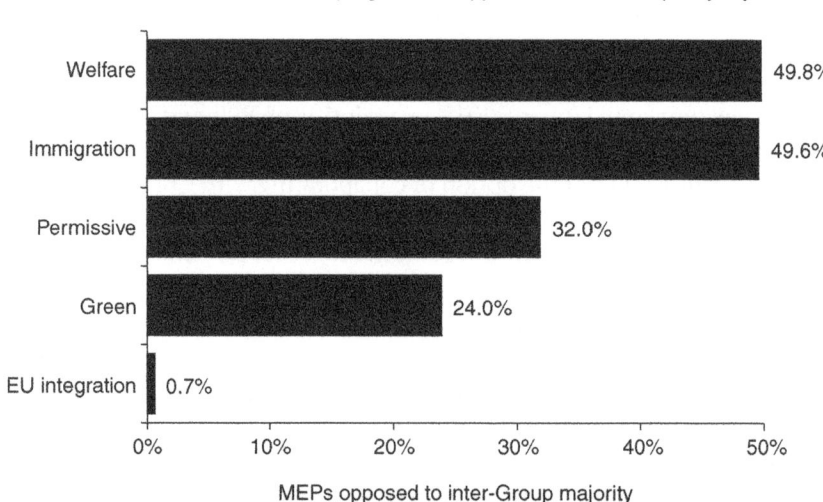

MEPs with national programmes opposed to inter-Group majority

MEPs opposed to inter-Group majority

Figure 7.1. Misrepresentation when People's Party and Socialists combine

Source: Calculated from data base of national party programmes for the 2009 EP election. See <http://www.EUProfiler.eu>.

immigration, there is a similarly high degree of misrepresentation. The EPP is more cohesive and thus able to tip the balance in favour of anti-immigrant measures and almost half of the MEPs are expected to vote against their national party programme. The virtual unanimity of the EPP in opposition to permissive measures enables it to determine the combined Groups' opposition to permissive legislation, against the stated position of three-quarters of Socialist MEPs. Combining in support of environmental legislation involves less misrepresentation by MEPs, because more than a third of EPP members are neutral and can more readily go along with pro-environment measures heavily supported by MEPs in the Socialist Group.

European integration is the one policy dimension in which aggregation reflects agreement between Party Groups. A black-red combination is more than 99 per cent in agreement on EU integration. The addition of Liberals shows 532 MEPs in favour of an ever closer Union and only three against. Support for more powers for the EU is consistent with the collective institutional interest of MEPs in having an impact on policy. If the agreement among parties was matched by that of their electorates, then Party Groups would, as the Maastricht Treaty claims, reflect the 'will' of Europe's citizens.

Consensus in the European Parliament is repressive; a cartel that fails to represent the divisions of Europe's citizens about whether an ever closer Union is desirable. Three-fifths of Europeans do not favour more integration; the median voter endorses leaving things as they are and a minority would actually like less integration. European voters cannot rely on parties that they vote for to represent their views when votes are taken in the European Parliament. The EP consensus downloads conflicts in representation to national parties and their electorates. This reconfigures the choice that voters have; it is between cartel parties and parties that protest against them. Electors who do not feel represented by what the European Parliament does can, as national citizens, vote for parties that challenge the European-level consensus.

8

Interdependence: How Policy Changes Politics

Policy makes politics and politics makes policy.

Theodore J. Lowi

There are two kinds of European countries; those that are small and know it and those that are small and don't.

A Belgian prime minister

Policy interdependence occurs when the actions of one government are necessarily affected by what other governments do. Interdependent policies differ from policies in such fields as health and education, which are the exclusive responsibility of national governments. Interdependent problems require cross-national co-operation, for example, railway tracks linking two countries. When countries vie to host the Olympics or attract big foreign investors, interdependence involves competition. It can also involve conflict, as in the fighting between successor states of the former Republic of Yugoslavia. Interdependence shifts the venue of politics from a closed domestic arena to a field in which national governments and other institutions, including the European Union, interact. In itself it is neither desirable nor undesirable. If there is a positive outcome, then interdependence creates collective goods; if the outcome is negative, as in the wars that have racked Europe in the past, the outcome is a collective evil.

Combatting crime is a classic function of national governments and in keeping with the EU's doctrine of subsidiarity, policing is a national responsibility. However, to combat trans-national drug smuggling and to apprehend criminals who flee their jurisdiction, national police forces require the co-operation of police in other countries. The evolution of Interpol, the shorthand name of the International Criminal Police Organization, illustrates how interdependence has led to the creation of a European and then a global institution to deal with trans-national crime. It was founded by European police authorities in 1914; its headquarters were initially in Vienna and are now in France. It represents its 190 national members with regional offices in Brussels for the European Commission and in New York for the United Nations.

Co-operation to deal with the challenge of interdependence depends on common interests; it does not require a common identity. The alliance of Nazi Germany and the Soviet Union in 1939 reflected a common interest not a shared identity, and the same was true of the alliance of the Soviet Union with the United Kingdom and the United States after Nazi Germany turned on it. The countries that founded the European Union were not giving up their national identity. They were giving recognition to the fact that nominal sovereignty had not saved them from defeat in the Second World War and interwar depression. They were abandoning the French tradition of mercantilism and the German commitment to *Nationalwirtschaft*, which assumed that national economies could prosper by avoiding trade with other countries. The EU's founders sought to promote peace and prosperity through a market in which a high level of trade created a high level of interdependence.

Interdependence changes both politics and policy. It can lead to co-operation for mutual advantage, for example, in building a bridge that crosses a river dividing two countries. When countries are unequal in their resources, then the better endowed country can impose conditions. Even though there are substantial inequalities between EU member states, the decisions it takes rely on consensus among a big majority of member states. In the absence of such a constraint, inequalities can be exploited by the stronger state, as Russia does when it interrupts the supply of fuel to Ukraine in order to influence its politics.

Interdependent policies challenge the idea of the state as sovereign, that is, a political institution that has a monopoly of power over what happens within a given territory. It forces a state to take into account how what happens outside its boundaries affects decisions taken within it. To ignore this does not protect a national government from external influences. It means that when the effects of the policies of other countries are felt domestically, as in the Eurozone crisis, they come as an unwelcome surprise.

Politics requires countries wanting to take collective action to develop political institutions that are effective across national boundaries. An institution can have a single purpose, such as the International Postal Union, or a broad range of functions, as does the EU. It can have little money and few legal powers, relying primarily on its ability to provide ideas and advice, as is the case with the Organisation for Economic Co-operation and Development (OECD), or it can have multiple functions, a substantial budget, and legal powers, as does the European Union.

In large European countries interdependence challenges national leaders to recognize that the problems that they face are bigger than they see themselves. The size of a country does not create immunity from the effects of interdependence; what is critical is its size in relation to other countries with which it must deal. Among British politicians the country's former great power status has obscured this essential fact and encouraged rhetoric about the sovereignty of Parliament and an all-powerful prime minister. David Cameron failed to understand this when he sought to dictate to other governments terms for dealing with the Eurozone crisis. By contrast, other large member states are pragmatically prepared to accept policy initiatives from Brussels when collective action at the European level can help resolve a problem that they face nationally. Thus, Poland, a big country by comparison with Lithuania and Belarus, recognizes that it is relatively small in relation to Germany and Russia.

For smaller member states interdependence has always been a fact of life. The choice is not between participating in an EU policy and making its own policy but between participating in policymaking in Brussels and being a bystander to policies decided in Berlin, Paris, or London. Leaders of the small states that constitute the bulk of the EU's membership know that decisions depend not only on what they want but also on the positions of bigger states. Thanks to EU membership, instead of being the weaker partner vis-a-vis a neighbour with much greater economic and military power, small states have legal equality with big states. When decisions are made in EU bodies, Ireland and Austria have a right to be at the table along with Britain and Germany.

Even if not a member of the European Union, countries must come to terms with the challenge of interdependence. The Norwegian government has twice negotiated membership in the European Union and its citizens have twice rejected membership at referendums. Yet because of the interdependence of Norway's economic and foreign policies with those of other European states, it has been a partner in the European Economic Area since 1992. The Area institutionalizes co-operation with the EU on unequal terms. An official Norwegian review justifies this as reflecting the reality of interdependence:

> Norway's relations with the EU are shaped by the need to find common solutions to transborder challenges related to the economy and development, migration, technology, climate change and the environment, resource management, globalization, peace, people-to-people contacts, etc. Some form of binding cooperation is required to respond to most of these challenges.

Norway has accepted more than 6,000 relatively minor EU measures since it entered association with the EU. In addition, the Norwegian Parliament has been asked to vote on 287 major new obligations which the EU agreed without Norwegian participation. Of these, 265 were adopted unanimously and the remainder by big majorities. The Report concludes: 'The last 20 years have shown clearly that the Norwegian authorities neither can nor wish to isolate Norway from the increasingly close and binding integration processes in the EU.'[1] In a complementary manner, Scandinavian countries that are EU member states do not want their EU membership to reduce their close and binding ties with Norway.

The European Union is now an integral part of the policy and politics of member states. Moreover, interdependence does not stop at the boundaries of the European Union; it has gone global. The value of the euro is affected by trading in Tokyo and New York as well as London and Frankfurt, and by credit rating agencies in the United States. The price of petrol that motorists pay reflects decisions made by oil-producing states that belong to the Organization of Petroleum Exporting Countries (OPEC).

I Interdependence without Consensus

The European Union has treaty powers and institutions that can deal with problems of interdependence. However, this is not a sufficient condition for collective action. The EU cannot act until there is a consensus among member states about what it should do. National governments are not elected to do what the European Commission wants. They depend on their national electorate to support their policies. Politics affects policy by imposing constraints on collective action. These constraints limit what the EU may do in fields such as social cohesion, immigration and multi-culturalism, and foreign and security policy.

Social cohesion stops at national borders. The EU's principle of *social cohesion* interprets interdependence as collective responsibility for the state to care for the welfare of others. The idea of *solidarité* was promoted by the French sociologist Emile Durkheim, who emphasized that society is much more than an aggregation of individuals; this theme is also found in organic Catholic philosophy. Similarly, the German Constitution describes the government as being a *sozialstaat* (social state) promoting social cohesion through welfare state policies. Consistent with the idea of citizenship, social cohesion has a bias in favour of equality. The absence of these continental terms in Anglo-American political discourse reflects the political priority it gives to individual freedom and individual economic choice. Margaret Thatcher gave extreme expression to this view when she declared, 'There is no such thing as society.'

The Treaty on the Functioning of the European Union describes social, economic, and territorial cohesion as necessary 'to promote the overall harmonious development of the Union' (Title XVIII). Social cohesion is expected not only to provide the 'glue' that binds citizens within a national society but also to strengthen an emerging European society. In the EU social cohesion justifies policies intended to reduce economic inequalities by providing financial benefits to regions less economically favoured because they are rural, geographically isolated, or have declining industries. The bulk of the EU budget goes to programmes of its Cohesion and Social Funds.

Financing social cohesion policies requires the transfer of money from better off countries, regions, and social groups to those that are worse off. The readiness of member states to transfer money depends on whether the principle is applied at the national or at the EU level. National governments use their taxing powers to raise money from higher-income citizens and regions and spend it for the benefit of less well off regions and poorer groups. Even though relatively less well off German regions are prosperous by the standards of Eastern Europe, the German government has spent hundreds of billions to promote social cohesion between West German regions and those in East Germany afflicted by the legacy of the Communist-controlled East German state.

Social solidarity tends to stop at national borders. Prosperous smaller EU member states lack the money to deal with the social disparities between themselves and less well off countries with bigger populations such as Poland and Romania. Bigger EU member states are unwilling to contribute the large amount of money that would be needed to increase social cohesion between the Union's best off and least well off states (see Table 3.1). In limiting their commitment to cross-national solidarity, better off EU member states have the endorsement of their citizens. A Eurobarometer survey in autumn 2010 (74.1) found that only 35 per cent of Europe's citizens endorsed solidarity among EU member states. The proportion was lower in older and more prosperous EU member states; only 26 per cent of Swedes and 17 per cent of Britons favoured the EU giving a high priority to solidarity between European countries.

The introduction of the euro not only recognized currency interdependence but also sought to promote social cohesion. Major structural differences in the political economies of member states were glossed over in the expectation that sharing a common currency would encourage or even force convergence between member states. In its first years the European Central Bank was successful in its primary goal of keeping inflation and interest rates down, but, as subsequent events have revealed, it was spectacularly unsuccessful in getting Mediterranean countries to adopt German standards of economic management. The Eurozone crisis has demonstrated the down side of interdependence: Germany and Greece are now locked together in a classic relation between lender and debtor—with all the conflict that goes with it.

Enlargement has greatly reduced social cohesion within the EU because of the gap in incomes between former Communist economies and Western

Europe. The median Gross Domestic Product per capita in older member states is more than three times that of new member states (see Table 3.1). Logically, the historic gap in income could be substantially reduced by more rapid economic growth in countries below the EU's mean standard of living. However, this is easier said than done. In order to reduce existing gaps, less well off countries would need a rate of growth that is three times higher than in the decade before the 2008 crisis.

More cultures, less solidarity. Cultural solidarity exists among a community of people who share an emotional sense of attachment as well as agreement on principles of behaviour. It does not require common citizenship. The Nordic Union institutionalizes a degree of solidarity between citizens of countries stretching from Finland to Iceland and differing in their histories and contemporary relationship with the European Union. When a British prime minister refers to the country's 'special relationship' with the United States, he or she is not signalling that Britain wants to become the 51st American state. Instead, the intention is to show British solidarity with other peoples of the English-speaking world. Distance is not a barrier to solidarity nor does proximity necessarily promote it. Britons have felt more in common with people on the other side of the globe in Australia than with neighbours on the other side of the English Channel.

European Union policies have greatly expanded the number and variety of national cultures now found within the European Union. Enlargement from 6 to 27 countries has created a political institution with 23 different official languages and national histories. Unlike the multi-national empires of the past, each of the national governments that constitutes the EU's domain has substantial political powers. A consensus of diverse countries is required before major steps can be taken towards an ever closer Union.

The single Europe market has brought people of different nationalities more closely into contact through the free movement of peoples as well as goods and services. Economic calculations rather than cultural affinities encourage people to leave lands with high unemployment to seek work in other countries. The result is movement between least similar countries, for example, between Portugal and Luxembourg or Romania and France. Germany, Britain, and Ireland have been major recipients of immigrants from lower-income EU member states such as Poland. However, this policy does not have the support of people who are national as well as European citizens. In older EU member states up to two-thirds of people think that priority should be given to national citizens over immigrants if jobs are scarce.[2]

Cultural diversity has increased the social distance between peoples sharing EU citizenship and has reduced solidarity. When the 2004 European Election Study asked how much trust respondents had in people from other member states, respondents expressed a lot of trust in people from the older member states. Swedes were trusted by as many as 68 per cent of respondents and the median level of trust was 56 per cent. By contrast, the median level of trust in people from new member states was 36 per cent. Moreover, the level of trust in each new member state was below the 47 per cent level of the least trusted old member state, Britain.

The EU's support for the free movement of peoples has made it a magnet for immigrants from low income countries and its democratic structures have made it a haven for individuals claiming refugee status from brutal regimes and failed states. Immigration is no longer about the movement of people who are 'like us', however that term is defined. Immigration from poorer countries in other continents that were once colonies of member states has particularly affected the United Kingdom, France, the Netherlands, Belgium, and Portugal. Immigrants come from North Africa to France, from Turkey to Germany, and from Pakistan, India, and the West Indies to Britain. In order to communicate with British citizens having the right to vote, the United Kingdom Electoral Commission now offers voters information in five EU languages and six from other continents: Arabic, Bengali, Chinese, Gujarati, Hindi, and Urdu.

The population of the European Union is now multi-continental in its diversity. The official EU statistical office, Eurostat, estimates that there are 39 million people living in a European country who were not born there. Of this group, half are legal residents from another continent, more than one-fifth are illegal immigrants from another continent; and just over one-quarter are citizens of another EU member state.

Politics is now challenging whether solidarity can be maintained in the face of increased multi-culturalism. Europeans are now more likely to see multi-culturalism rather than economic differences as the greatest source of tension in their society.[3] In the European Quality of Life Survey, two-fifths show a lot of concern about racial and ethnic differences in their society and 31 per cent think there is a lot of tension between religions. The two attitudes are highly correlated, reflecting the fact that many minorities differ from the population of the European country in which they live on a combination of racial, ethnic, and/or religious grounds. The tension is not derived from older divisions within European societies between churchgoers and anti-clericals or English and Irish. Nor is tension especially associated with intra-European immigration.

Tensions are associated with immigrants from Muslim societies such as North Africa, Turkey, the Indian subcontinent, and Indonesia. Since intercontinental immigrants tend to seek work in high-income countries, these tensions tend to be higher in prosperous EU countries. In the Netherlands and Italy almost half of the public see racial and religious tensions as high. By contrast, in low-income countries such as Bulgaria and Latvia, which have historic ethnic minorities but few recent immigrants, only one in ten report a lot of tension.

There is growing opposition within member states to the values of diversity and multi-culturalism that the European Commission promotes. There is a substantial majority against multi-culturalism among those favouring further EU integration as well as among those wanting less. A total of 74 per cent of European Election Study respondents think immigrants should be required to adopt the customs of their host country. In addition, there is also a majority, 56 per cent, in favour of substantially reducing immigration, an action that would challenge EU policy on the free movement of peoples.

Foreign policy: too many voices. Defence is the classic example of interdependence, since a country's security is defined in relation to other states. Neutrality can be maintained only if it is respected by stronger powers—and the Second World War showed this is usually not the case. Lacking the population and economic resources of major military powers, most European states have sought security by joining a military alliance led by a major power. In a military alliance, all national partners are pledged to collective action in their mutual defence, but the relationship among them is unequal. Most partners depend for their security on the strongest military partner.

Although the EU has territorial boundaries, it does not have an army. This is not because the EU lacks the resources; collectively, it has the economic resources of a major military power and almost 200 million more people than the United States. The lack is due to politics determining policy—or the absence thereof. Consensus has been chronically lacking in security and foreign policy. During the Cold War the defence of Europe against Soviet troops was located in the other Brussels, the headquarters of the Council of the North Atlantic Treaty Organization (NATO). The end of the Cold War has radically reduced the threat of military invasion on Europe's eastern frontier. Nonetheless, European countries have continued to maintain commitment to NATO as their primary force for national defence. Although EU member states are a majority of NATO's members, six EU countries—Finland, Sweden, Austria, Ireland, Cyprus, and Malta—do not belong. NATO gives a high priority to a command structure that fits many national units into a multi-national force. Formally, NATO is an alliance, but unlike the EU it is a military alliance in which the strongest military power, the United States, is dominant.

The Maastricht Treaty made a highly qualified commitment to the EU 'eventually framing a common defence policy, which might in time lead to a common defence'. This has led to the establishment of a multi-national European Rapid Reaction Force. The EU can despatch in its name a few dozen, a few hundred, or a few thousand uniformed personnel to post-conflict situations in places close to the EU's borders such as Kosovo and further afield to places such as the Democratic Republic of the Congo.

The EU has been unable to develop a substantial security policy because member states do not agree about the use of force. In Afghanistan and Iraq, European states have disagreed about whether to follow American leadership. Some national governments have been willing to participate, if only symbolically, while others are unwilling to do so. When the Libyan uprising occurred in 2011, the issue was discussed in the European Council but no EU action could be taken because of disagreements there. The French and British national governments committed their air forces to protect the insurgents, but Germany abstained from engagement. Shortcomings in the capability of the European forces made American assistance necessary.

Notwithstanding attempts by the European Commission to develop a common European energy policy, national governments have preferred to make their own arrangements. Energy policy has a security dimension because 19 member states import more than half their energy and 8 more import between a quarter and one-half of their annual energy needs. The source of energy has political implications. Russia is the main source of EU energy, accounting for one-third of the imported energy heating European homes and serving European industries. Vladimir Putin has been prepared to exert Russian pressure on countries dependent on Russian energy. Middle Eastern countries account for an additional third of the oil that Europeans consume and one-quarter of the gas; they are politically high risk countries. For example, the Nord Stream pipeline connecting Russia's Gazprom with Germany by an underwater pipeline creates anxiety among bypassed EU member states in the Baltic region. In Southern Europe there have been controversies between EU member states about bypassing Russia by means of the Nabucco pipeline.

The everyday conduct of foreign policy involves talk rather than troops. Every EU member state has embassies that look after its national interests in countries of central concern. The embassies of large states such as Britain, France, and Germany are prominent in the capitals of major countries and in international organizations. Sweden plays an active role as a broker between big powers. The Lisbon Treaty created the office of High Representative of the EU as the spokesperson of the European Council. It also authorized a diplomatic corps, the European External Action Service, staffed by existing EU personnel engaged in external affairs and by mid-career diplomats seconded from member states. However, the EU also has significant relations with non-member states concerning trade, development, and economic policy. None of these policies is in the hands of the new diplomatic corps; they remain the responsibility of other EU Directorates.

The voice of the EU is muffled in foreign policy because major member states differ in what they want said. The very low political status of the first EU High Representative for Foreign Affairs and Security Policy, Lady Catherine Ashton, is acceptable to major states because they want to continue speaking for themselves in foreign policy. In the absence of agreement, EU diplomats are limited in what they can represent as a European position. If they attempt to speak on behalf of all member states without prior agreement, they risk having their claims shot down by national embassies on guard against being upstaged by an EU spokesperson. Nor is there demand from public opinion for the EU to replace national governments in formulating foreign policy. When a Eurobarometer survey in autumn 2010 asked people to choose four priorities for EU attention from a list of twelve, having the EU speak with one voice in foreign policy came tenth and only 17 per cent described it as an important priority.

II The Globalization of Europe

A century ago European states saw themselves as the centre of the world. Calling the twentieth-century wars that started in Europe world wars is an unwelcome reminder of Europe's global impact then. The largest states were empires that had colonies on other continents. Britain could boast that the sun never set on its worldwide empire, which ruled more than one-fifth of the world's population. Changes since then have brought about a reversal of roles. The globalization of politics, economics, and communications has resulted in Europe no longer being the centre of world politics. Today, Europe is a region in the global system and the European Union is a regional institution sharing policy concerns within a global network of hundreds of states and intergovernmental, supra-national, and non-state regional and global organizations. To project its views globally, the EU now has representative offices in one hundred countries from Afghanistan to Zimbabwe.

The metaphor of levels of government does not apply to global politics, for there is no top tier. European states are now embedded in an irregular polyhedron with many sides. Each side represents a different policy concern of the states involved. The overall pattern is irregular, because of differences in the institutional resources and political clout that supra-national organizations have. Organizations that are truly global in their scope are often weaker, because of the difficulties in securing agreement among diverse members. This is the chronic problem of the United Nations. Global institutions that have a narrow range of functions can be effective within limits; for example, the International Monetary Fund loans money to countries temporarily in financial difficulties but it cannot regulate the actions of national economies that lead to these difficulties.

Policy shrinks and stretches the definition of Europe. The elastic character of Europe's boundaries is shown by the varying number of states belonging to nominally European institutions. Even though policymaking within the

Eurozone impacts the whole of the EU and beyond, less than two-thirds of the EU's members currently belong to the Eurozone and there is an active debate about whether it would be better for all concerned to shrink rather than expand its membership. Insofar as the Eurozone is representative of Europe, this is because its members include countries that have been prudent in managing their national finances and those that have been profligate.

The need for collective military security has stretched the definition of Europe across the Atlantic. Confronted with Soviet troops occupying neighbouring states, European countries welcomed the founding of what is rightly called the North Atlantic Treaty Organization. The United States makes by far the biggest national contribution to NATO. The second largest military force is that of Turkey, which was admitted to guard Europe's southern flank long before it was given the status of a candidate for EU membership. Since the collapse of the Soviet Union, Europe is no longer NATO's only theatre of operation. The United States gives priority to military challenges outside Europe. In doing so, it forms coalitions of the willing. Some EU members of NATO are willing to join its coalitions while others are not.

The Council of Europe, founded in 1949, was encouraged into being by the rhetorical enthusiasm of Winston Churchill for a United States of Europe. It also reflects the resistance of Churchill and other leaders of national governments to the creation of an institution with effective powers to act. The result is an organization capable of talking and issuing opinions about a wide range of issues in the broad field of human rights, but without the legal, financial, or administrative resources of the EU. Its membership of 47 states includes all 27 EU members; Turkey and Balkan countries with which the EU is negotiating relationships; mini-states such as Liechtenstein and San Marino; and Russia. The European Court of Human Rights was established in parallel to enforce individual political and civil rights as specified in the European Convention of Human Rights.

Since the fall of the Berlin Wall, political institutions have extended the nominal boundaries of Europe far beyond the limits of member states. The European Bank for Reconstruction and Development (EBRD) provides finance for countries that have long-term economic problems due to the legacy of the Communist bloc's command economies. Because the demand for development funding is not geographically restricted, the EBRD has extended its membership to include Turkey, four Middle East countries ranging from Morocco to Jordan, and Mongolia. Member countries providing funds for the EBRD include Australia, Japan, and Mexico. The United Nations Economic Commission for Europe stretches across continents too. Its 56 members include not only Central Asian successor states of the Soviet Union but also the United States and Canada.

The Organization for Security and Co-operation in Europe (OSCE) was founded after the fall of the Berlin Wall to undertake conflict prevention, crisis management, and the promotion of freedom and democracy. Since most conflicts and challenges to democracy are found outside the European Union, the OSCE includes successor states of the Soviet Union and of the Republic of Yugoslavia. The OSCE's partners include Islamic countries such as Algeria and Egypt as well as Asian countries at the back door of Russia such as South Korea and Japan. Even though co-operation on security is notionally a major responsibility of the European Union, the OSCE head office is in Vienna rather than Brussels.

Europe goes global. All EU member states are UN members, but the creation of many small states in the wake of colonial independence has reduced Europe to one-seventh of the UN's total membership. The culture of the UN is that of developing countries distant from Europe in many senses. Insofar as values and priorities are proclaimed on such issues as human rights, they are by definition universal rather than distinctively European. However, the UN lacks the institutions to enforce these rights. The European Union has observer status at the UN. This entitles it to participate in many UN discussions and conventions, but it is not recognized as a member state. Britain and France jealously guard their privileged status as permanent members of the UN Security Council and have no wish to sacrifice their places to a European Union representative.

In international economic organizations such as the International Monetary Fund and the World Bank, EU countries are also in a minority. The governing boards of both the Fund and the Bank include a number of European countries, but they sit there as representatives of national governments and the attention paid to their opinions is heavily weighted by their financial contribution. The EU pays no contribution. By convention, the head of the IMF is a European and of the World Bank an American, but the choice is made by negotiations among national governments in which major developing countries such as China, India, and Brazil are demanding a bigger role.

The globalization of finance means that European governments borrow money from other countries outside Europe as well as from their own citizens and institutions. Interest rates are set by global market pressures rather than by the fiat of national governments; countries that are rated as risky by non-governmental organizations pay more to finance their deficits. The denomination of loans in euros creates a complication because the value of the euro fluctuates in relation to other major currencies, such as the dollar, the Swiss franc, and the yen. Banks and speculators express confidence or anxiety about Eurozone economic policies by buying it or selling it short. The double-edged sword of interdependence is shown by the swings in the euro's foreign exchange value. The exchange rate of one euro to the US dollar has fluctuated between

82 cents and $1.59. Fluctuations are influenced by decisions and indecisions taken in other countries and continents as well as within the Eurozone.

EU treaties make trade the one policy area in which the EU actively represents its member states as a whole in the international economy. It is a full member of the World Trade Organization (WTO). There it can advocate maintaining policies deemed of advantage within Europe, such as protecting Europe's subsidized agricultural products from international competition. The European Commission also has the staff and the authority to negotiate trade agreements with developing countries and with major trading countries such as the United States and Japan.

Globalization and Europeanization. The European Union is pulled two ways by the pressures of globalization and nationalization. On the one hand, developments outside the borders of member states create pressures to engage with countries that are not eligible for EU membership, whether because they are part of the undemocratic fringes of Europe or they are on other continents. Concurrently, political disagreements within the EU make it difficult for the EU to act as the spokesperson for a united Europe. Member states formulate their own policies in alliance with other countries within or outside Europe.

The only major institution that consists exclusively of EU member states, the European Central Bank, fails to include all member states (Table 8.1). In most nominally European institutions, EU members participate as national governments along with governments of countries that are not EU member states. EU member states make up less than half the members of the European Bank for Reconstruction and Development and of the Organization for Security and Co-operation in Europe. Even though most members of NATO are

Table 8.1. Interdependence of European states

	Number of members		
	EU countries	Non-EU	EU as % total
ORGANIZATIONS STRETCHING EUROPE'S BOUNDARIES			
North Atlantic Treaty Organization	21	6	78
European Central Bank	17	n.a.	100
Council of Europe	27	20	57
OSCE	27	29	48
EBRD	27	36	43
INTERNATIONAL ORGANIZATIONS			
World Trade Organization	27	129	17
International Monetary Fund	27	161	14
World Bank	27	161	14
Interpol	27	163	14
United Nations	27	166	14

Note: European Central Bank: percentage of EU members in ECB.

European countries, they cannot compare in importance with the military power of the United States. Whereas European states are individual members of major international organizations, the best the EU can claim is observer status. Only in the World Trade Organization does the EU normally speak for Europe.

Policy makes politics. For interdependent problems within the collective boundaries of member states, as long as treaties give the EU authority to act, Brussels can take the lead. But when interdependence extends to other countries and institutions, the EU's treaty powers are insufficient to give it the capacity to determine outcomes. In discussions about policy, European Union institutions must seek agreement not only among its member states but also with states on other continents, multi-national corporations, international non-governmental organizations, and intergovernmental organizations with far broader memberships but fewer and weaker powers than the EU has.

Politics decides how policy is made. International politics is usually managed by exchanges between states, and major EU members such as the United Kingdom, France, and Germany can engage in bilateral discussions with other countries and make their voices heard in intergovernmental organizations. While the White House can now ring the President of the European Council to ask what the EU position is on a major issue, the clarity of the answer will depend on whether major member states agree on both the substance of a policy and whether the European Council President or national governments should speak for European member states in dialogues with Washington.

The commitment of member states to an EU agreement is not the same as the commitment of its citizens. There is widespread popular awareness that Europeanization and globalization are affecting the lives of ordinary citizens. Because the economy and domestic security are primary national responsibilities, citizens look to their national government to deal with these problems, whether they are deemed to originate in Brussels, Washington, or something as hard to locate as the international financial system. Moreover, citizens of democratic states retain the right to give or withhold commitment to what their national government decides. For most of the half billion people caught up in Europeanization and globalization, where a problem is dealt with is less important than whether it is dealt with effectively.

9

The Future of Europe: An Ever Looser Union?

We are here to undertake a common task—not to negotiate for our own national advantage but to seek it in the advantage of all.

Jean Monnet, *Memoirs*

The root of Europe's political crisis: the necessity and impossibility of integration.

Mark Leonard, European Council on Foreign Relations

Interdependence stimulates demands to deepen and broaden the EU's powers, thus advancing an ever closer Union. It is welcome in Brussels because it shows the twenty-first century need for collective action in a world very different from what the EU's founders could have foreseen. National governments struggling with issues beyond their capacity can welcome the EU dealing with such collective problems as the regulation of multi-national companies in hopes that this will be to the advantage of all.

Before the European Union can act, there must be political agreement. The checks in a system designed for six countries have become greater as the EU has expanded and become more diverse. The obstacles to securing a consensus have led an advocate of collective action, Mark Leonard, to worry that the EU cannot continue to achieve the degree of integration necessary to meet the challenges of interdependence effectively.

If further integration is considered undesirable, as Eurosceptics argue, then the veto that politics places on policy is acceptable. It protects the right of each member state to adopt whatever policy it considers appropriate to deal with problems facing it. For example, national governments can maintain their energy supplies by bilateral negotiations with Russia and with Middle Eastern states; by multilateral co-operation with non-EU member states to build new pipelines; and by domestic initiatives to develop renewable sources of energy. When military action is the issue, member states can act independently of the EU, dividing into coalitions of the willing and of the unwilling. Co-operation outside EU institutions does not deny interdependence; it encourages the development of an ever looser Union.

The greater the extent of interdependence, the sooner events outside the control of Brussels are likely to disrupt the ties that maintain a policy equilibrium in place. Each of the pillars of EU policy is vulnerable to external shocks. The crisis of the Eurozone is a textbook example of how ECB policies appeared stable until an economic crisis starting in New York deprived the EU of the luxury of defending the status quo. Security problems in Europe's neighbouring states can blow up unexpectedly and the porousness of the EU's borders can result in an unwelcome spillover of immigrants and refugees that causes political problems within member states.

Because the challenges of interdependence are too big to ignore, the critical question is not whether the European Union will respond but how it should do so. To act effectively, the Commission must have the capacity—political, legal, and financial—to make a positive impact. The EU has greatly expanded the scope of its formal powers, but it has not always expanded its capacity to exercise these powers effectively. Nor has an ever more diverse Union found it easy to secure consensus about what it should do. This chapter suggests that when consensus is lacking, there is a pragmatic alternative, enhanced cooperation by coalitions of willing member states. When major EU policies impose immediate and visible costs, national governments should not assume that their citizens will be committed to whatever is agreed in Brussels. Popular commitment to an ever closer Union can best be secured by putting fresh treaties to the test of a pan-European referendum.

I Limits to Capacity

While the principle of European integration is open-ended, it cannot be unlimited in practice. Theories of European integration rarely take into account limits to the EU's capacity to broaden and deepen its activities. Likewise, the EU's Copenhagen criteria for admitting new members do not include the requirement that the EU must have the capacity to absorb an applicant country, for example, sufficient money for the long-term funding of its economic development or the ability to get rid of corruption in an applicant country where it has long been endemic. The EU can set ambitious targets for what Europe should be like in 2020, but if these goals are beyond the EU's capacity to achieve, then instead of promoting an ever closer Union, unrealistic goals will reveal an even weaker Union. Stating goals without the legal authority, money, and political will to act effectively creates policy deficits. These include deficits in democracy; in the rule of law; and in the functioning of economies, and imply limits to further EU enlargement.

Deficits in the EU's current capacity. The deficit most often ascribed to the European Union is a democratic deficit. The electoral inputs that Europe's citizens can make are limited by comparison with the influence that voters have on national governments. In 2009 the German Constitutional Court moved this issue from the realm of academic debate to that of practical politics. It did so by a decision that placed a question mark over the extent to which the German government could cede authority to the European Union, because the latter does not have democratic practices up to the standard that the German Constitution requires of the Federal Republic. Even though the Court has not annulled any EU measure, it has drawn a line between accepting EU policies within the framework of existing treaties and new powers that the German state should approve only after its Parliament has given its approval. The Court's scrutiny of the constitutionality of EU decisions risks an agreement that a German chancellor accepts in Brussels being upset by a decision of the German Federal Court in Karlsruhe.

The election of a President of Europe is frequently proposed as a means of reducing the democratic deficit. For example, the German finance minister, Wolfgang Schauble, has suggested this as a way to balance the increased powers that the EU has claimed over the fiscal policies of national governments. However, any plan to do so would be confronted by the lack of a democratic system of counting votes. To elect a President on the basis of one person, one vote, one value, as is done in France, would be unacceptable to the many member states whose electorates are too small to have any influence. To elect a President by an electoral college would be unacceptable to big states if it reproduced the inequality that degressive proportionality creates in the European Parliament. A requirement for the winning candidate to secure the endorsement of an absolute majority of citizens and states would require two or three rounds of voting before a winner emerged.

Locking in national democracy is a major EU concern, since the majority of EU members were new democracies when they joined. The EU does not have the power to expel a member state that takes an undemocratic turn but it can charge it with a serious and persistent breach of democratic values and suspend some of its rights. However, this power has not been used because the EU has an enforcement deficit. When the Austrian People's Party formed a coalition government in 2000 with the Freedom Party, which was led by a politician with neo-Nazi sympathies, the most the EU could do was practise 'quasi-ostracism'. Member states announced that they would not hold bilateral negotiations with the Austrian government, a diplomatic move that did not affect Austria's participation in multilateral EU institutions. The problem was resolved within Austria by a split in the Freedom Party.

Hungarians concerned today about the removal of democratic protections by the Viktor Orban government look abroad for help. Freedom House, an international non-governmental organization, can denounce the threat of the Putinization of Hungary, while the EU is circumspect in confronting such conditions. It has expressed concern about the possible threats to freedom in new Hungarian laws but it lacks the political capacity to impose effective sanctions on a Hungarian government reducing checks and balances central to a democratic political system. In Romania the optimist says that the battle between the president and the prime minister about impeachment does not threaten to upset its political system, but rather reflects the maintenance of a system of bad governance.

The rule of law is of particular importance for the European Union, because the EU's chief policy resource is the making of laws that national governments are expected to implement. However, if national officials show favouritism in administering policies or corruption in allocating EU funds this undermines EU policy. In its 2010 Annual Report the European Court of Auditors complained that methods for controlling the national expenditure of EU funds were still only partially effective. In consequence, about 4.5 billion euros was spent in ways that did not comply with EU laws.

Concerns about corruption in Bulgaria and Romania resulted in their admission being delayed from 2004 to 2007. The two countries were then admitted on the condition that they continued to reduce corruption. However, this has not happened. In 2007 each had a rating on the Transparency International Corruption Perceptions Index below that of all older member states. Since then, their ratings have fallen further. On the 10-point Index, Romania has dropped to 3.6 and Bulgaria has dropped even lower to 3.3. Although each country is entitled to receive large amounts of EU funding on the basis of their needs, the way grants have been administered has led to the suspension of payments of hundreds of millions of euros pending investigation into evidence of corrupt disbursement.

The EU's inability to enforce the rule of law in new member states is paralleled by its lack of the capacity to enforce it in older member states. Although Italy is a founder member of the EU, it suffers from chronic government corruption; its Transparency International rating of 3.9 is below that of 24 member states. The corruption assessment of Greece is below that of Romania. Yet Greece was successful in having its fraudulent statistics accepted by the European Central Bank until the international bond market caught up with it.

Maintaining a functioning economy was included in the Copenhagen criteria because of difficulties that countries formerly part of the Communist bloc had with establishing an economic system suited to the single European market. The Eurozone crisis has shown that older member states such as Greece, Ireland, and Portugal have difficulties in maintaining a functioning economy too. Their difficulties have arisen *because* they are members of the Eurozone. Their integration in a single European monetary system has turned their national problems into a crisis of the European Union as a whole, as richer Eurozone countries are now faced with the cost of bailing out econ-omies that they had previously accepted as up to the EU's standard.

The Treaty on Economic Stability is intended to be the big step toward political Union that its sponsors aspired to, albeit the path has been different from and far more costly than the sponsors of the euro expected. Even though it increases the formal capacity of EU institutions, there is still a deficit in capacity, starting with foreknowledge. In order to hold national governments to the obligation of balancing their budget, EU technocrats will require fore-sight that economic forecasters have previously lacked. A budget deficit can be controlled only if the forecast of next year's expenditure is not underestimated and of next year's revenue is not overestimated. The political incentives to adopt rosy scenarios are strong and economists in Brussels and Frankfurt are not well placed to see through the smoke and mirrors that national finance ministries can use to push optimism about the future. EU institutions do not have enough money in hand to meet the potential claims of refinancing all of the Eurozone's troubled economies and there is pressure from Northern Euro-pean capitals to limit the sums committed to stabilizing the finances of troubled Mediterranean states. Whether EU member states have the political will to enforce the Treaty's rules remains to be seen. The International Monet-ary Fund has been brought in as a partner with EU institutions to strengthen that will and to share the responsibility for setting unwelcome conditions on how troubled member states should manage their national economies.

There are question marks over the legal status of a document that calls itself a Treaty in most European languages but in German is described by the conveniently ambiguous word *Vertrag*, which can refer to a contract or a treaty. The Stability Treaty has not been approved as EU treaties normally are by a unanimous vote of all 27 member states. The 'treaty-like' character of the emergency agreement is tacitly recognized by the inclusion in its final paragraph of a call for its substantive content to be incorporated into the EU's legal framework within five years.

Whatever its status in EU law, a treaty is not the same as an act of a national parliament. When national leaders face their national citizens they must justify in national terms why measures to cut spending and raise taxes are necessary. Although the EU does not claim authority over the health, educa-tion, and pensions programmes of member states, if big savings are required in order to meet Treaty demands for a balanced budget, then spending cuts will have to be made in these very popular domestic programmes. At this juncture, political difficulties loom large, because the Economic Stability Treaty imposes visible costs up front in pursuit of putative longer-term benefits.

Difficulties in the enforcement of the Stability Treaty are not the fault of weak leadership. They arise because Eurozone countries in economic difficulty are democracies, and their governments are accountable to their parliament and electorate as well as to EU technocrats. A June 2012 survey of eleven countries that had signed the Economic Stability Pact found that in ten countries most citizens wanted their national government to retain authority over economic and budget policy rather than transfer more authority to the European Union. The majority in favour of protecting national control was as high as 75 per cent in Sweden, and majorities in troubled Portugal as well as vulnerable Spain and Italy also favoured national governments keeping control of major economic decisions. On average 57 per cent favoured national control as against 37 per cent ready to cede more authority to the EU. The one exception is Germany. Since Germans see the EU as extending German practices of economic management to other countries, an absolute majority favoured Brussels doing so.[1]

Limits to enlargement. When a country is a candidate for membership, the EU has the capacity to impose conditions that it should meet in order to be accepted. While some conditions concern technical matters such as bringing commercial codes into harmony with the single European market, conditions can also require changes in practices of governance that fail to meet the EU's Copenhagen criteria. Whether these conditions can be met depends on the capacity of applicant countries as well as on the EU's ability to enforce conditions.

Five countries—Iceland, Macedonia, Montenegro, Serbia, and Turkey—are currently candidates for EU admission, the final stage in the process of gaining admission to membership. In addition, Albania, Bosnia & Herzegovina, and Kosovo are officially recognized as potential candidates for membership. The Balkan countries are adjacent to Croatia, which will become the EU's 28th member state in July 2013, while Turkey not only borders three EU member states but also Iraq, Iran, Syria, and the Caucasus.

The limit to further EU enlargement is not geography but the extent to which potential members, with the exception of Iceland, fall short of the EU's Copenhagen criteria for membership (Table 9.1). Technical assistance can be offered to potential members in hopes that this will raise their political standards, but, as Bulgaria and Romania demonstrate, neither foreign aid nor the promise of EU membership can buy good governance. If new members do not rapidly rise to EU standards the admission of countries that fail to meet the EU's current standards for democracy, the rule of law, and the economy risks creating a two-tier European Union.

Freedom House rates five countries—Macedonia, Turkey, Albania, Bosnia & Herzegovina, and Kosovo—as only partly free and Serbia and Montenegro are very new additions to its category of democratic political systems. Shortcomings of the political institutions of these countries reflect armed ethnic strife following the collapse of Yugoslavia. In Bosnia & Herzegovina and in Kosovo, a continuing presence of European troops is needed to prevent a recurrence of ethnic conflicts that have left unresolved scars.

Table 9.1. Potential EU member states evaluated

	Freedom House	GDP/cap €	Corruption
Candidate countries			
Iceland	Free	31,700	8.5
Montenegro	Free	5,114	3.7
Serbia	Free	4,143	3.5
Turkey	Partly free	7,500	4.4
Macedonia	Partly free	3,300	4.1
Potential candidates			
Bosnia & Herzegovina	Partly free	3,467	3.2
Albania	Partly free	2,891	3.3
Kosovo	Partly free	2,405	2.8
Median EU states			
Old EU 15	All free	33,500	7.8
2004–7 entrants	All free	11,000	5.2

Sources: Freedom House rating, 2012, <http://www.freedomhouse.org>. Corruption: Transparency International 2011, <http://www.transparency.org>; least corrupt: 10; most corrupt: 1. GDP per capita in euros: Eurostat 2011 and World Bank 2010.

On Transparency International's Corruption Index, the majority of applicant countries are graded as corrupt in the absolute sense. Except for Iceland, none has a corruption rating near that of the median country that entered the EU in 2004. The ratings of Turkey and Macedonia bracket them with Italy and Croatia, while corruption in Serbia and Montenegro has the ambiguous claim of being no worse than Greece. Three potential candidates—Albania, Bosnia & Herzegovina, and Kosovo—are at or below the EU's 'worst practice' standard of Bulgaria.

Because the Communist economy of Yugoslavia was much more open than Soviet-style command economies, the transition of its successor states to a functioning market economy has been less difficult than in post-Soviet states. However, most were among the poorer republics of Yugoslavia and years of ethnic strife have imposed further costs. Thus, the per capita GDP of potential member states is also low. The figure for the median would-be member state, Bosnia & Herzegovina, is less than one-third that of the median 2004 entrant, and barely one-tenth that of the median old EU member state. Moreover, three countries, Macedonia, Albania, and Kosovo, are poorer still. If admitted, seven applicant countries would be entitled to major claims on EU funds to promote social cohesion. Since the combined population of the applicant states is equal to that of Spain and Poland and the applicants' living standards are much lower, they would have a substantial displacement effect on funds that existing member states receive. Income inequality within these countries is an additional barrier to social cohesion. The Gini Index of income inequality is as high as 43 in Turkey and 44 in Macedonia, a third above the EU average.

A pragmatic evaluation of Turkey as an EU member state emphasizes limits to the European Union's capacity to absorb new members. Its population is bigger than any EU country except Germany and on current demographic trends will surpass Germany in about a decade. Because its Gross Domestic Product per capita is less than one-quarter that of the median old EU member state, if Turkey were admitted the EU could only finance its entitlement to funds at the expense of existing poorer member states. Turkey also falls short of meeting Copenhagen criteria. Freedom House's evaluation of Turkey as partly free reflects the charges and counter-charges of subverting the constitution that are exchanged between the secular army, which has intermittently controlled the government in recent decades, and a popularly elected government with Islamist inclinations. The Turkish government is quick to jail critics on vague charges of bringing the state into disrepute. Even though Turkey is a secular state, because a significant proportion of its population are practising Muslims, this has encouraged opposition in member states opposed to any extension of multi-culturalism. While the EU is unwilling to reject Turkey's application for membership, it is equally unwilling to accept it. The EU signed an agreement of association with Turkey in 1963, but did not accept it as a candidate for membership until 1999 and its application is not about to be acted upon.

Whatever happens to the current cluster of EU potential members, the challenge of interdependence remains. The EU maintains the European Economic Area as a form of quasi-membership for countries that it would welcome but that do not plan membership, such as Norway, and Switzerland is the subject of special arrangements. Russia and Ukraine, now neighbours of member states, are too big to be ignored, but they fall far short of Copenhagen criteria in democracy, the rule of law, corruption, and the way their economies function. The current EU policy of encouraging talks about EU membership without granting membership risks frustrating neighbours.

II Co-operation without Unanimity

While increased interdependence among EU member states encourages an expansion of the EU's role, increased diversity makes it harder to secure agreement for one-size-fits-all policies that are required to maintain uniform progress towards an ever closer Union. Disagreements are not limited to minor issues or provoked by a single state. On major issues of economic policy, there is a classic conflict of interest between debtor and lender countries. There are also conflicts of principle within European countries about the best way to achieve economic growth while dealing with deficits.

When there is disagreement, one option is to avoid taking action, however necessary, especially action that would require a new treaty subject to approval by every member state. An alternative is to embody the expansion of EU powers in documents that are treaty-like but not subject to the risky process of unanimous consent. If a measure can be approved by a Qualified Majority Vote, then countries that do not share the consensus view will be expected to implement it with little or no political commitment. A third alternative, provided for in the Lisbon Treaty, is that a member state can withdraw from the European Union. However, this nuclear option would raise a host of problems of transition for the country wanting to leave the EU, and it would be negotiating from a weak position vis-a-vis Brussels.

What works for whom? The logic of European integration is that it advances by adopting collective policies that benefit all member states. However, whether a policy advances European integration is of little consequence to Europeans. People are first of all national citizens and they look to their national government to produce effective policies to deal with problems that have visible effects nationally. Governments that are accountable to their national electorate can give priority to EU policies when this provides pragmatic benefits. For example, small states prefer discussions in Brussels, where they participate with big states, rather than having important policies decided in Franco-German summits from which they are excluded.

A pragmatic approach recommends that national governments evaluate EU measures in terms of their effectiveness without regard for their consequences for European integration. A pragmatic analysis of a proposal's consequences can identify the distribution of costs and benefits between countries. Alternatively, it may give priority to the distribution of costs and benefits between social groups, for example, workers and employers. However, evaluating EU proposals along left versus right lines is a recipe for disagreement. The division of national governments in the European Council and Council of Ministers between left, right, and centre makes the achievement of a super-majority unlikely, and a European Parliament majority normally requires avoiding or overcoming divisions along left-right partisan lines.

Whether co-operation is possible is a question of politics. It is the job of Commission staff to anticipate who will be affected by a proposal and to carry out discussions that lead to the removal of features that will cause opposition and strengthen features that will mobilize support. Insofar as the effect of a measure is limited, it can then be approved by the Committee of Permanent Representatives without political controversy. However, major EU policies by definition have a wide-ranging impact and identifiable costs and benefits are unlikely to be equally distributed among member states. In such circumstances unanimity is difficult to achieve.

In default of agreement in Brussels, member states can look elsewhere for help. British leaders normally look to Washington, whereas French and German leaders may turn to each other. To deal with problems of the international economy, discussions across continents are required. Following the 2008 economic crisis, a G-20 Economic Forum was established. Its members included the four largest EU member states; 15 countries on other continents; and, as sponsor of the euro, the European Union. However, the Global Forum quickly showed the twin vices of international groups: a lack of consensus about policies and a lack of institutions, money, and treaty powers to carry out any recommendations that were arrived at.

Coalitions of the willing. If EU member states disagree about what to do, this need not result in inaction. Enhanced co-operation offers countries that want to go further the opportunity of doing so without hindrance from hesitant member states.[2] Differentiated integration allows countries that opt out of co-operation to regard themselves as winners just as much as countries that opt in. Its procedures can create two coalitions of the willing. One will consist of countries that adopt a policy that they consider necessary and beneficial, while the other consists of countries that dislike it and do not have to adopt it. The outcome is thus very different from a policy that achieves uniformity by binding losers and winners together. It also differs from a situation in which a minority vetoes a policy that many countries want to put into effect.

The effect of enhanced co-operation is to expand the capacity of the EU through measures that have a 'Europeanizing' effect on some countries and may have a 'de-Europeanizing' effect on others. It offers countries that have joined the European Union at different times for different reasons an alternative between marching lock step on a journey towards an ever closer Union or abandoning EU membership because they do not want to go further towards an unwanted or unknown destination.

EU treaties set out how member states can agree to disagree. Enhanced co-operation requires a minimum of one-third of member states to work together; approval by the European Parliament; and a Commission proposal for enhanced co-operation in economic policy, justice, or home affairs together with unanimous approval by the European Council on matters of foreign and security policy. Enhanced co-operation cannot be applied to every measure that the EU adopts, for example, such collective goods as the admission of new member states. The flexibility of enhanced co-operation means that it can be applied ad hoc to break a deadlock when insistence on uniformity would result in the EU doing nothing.

In one or another form, enhanced co-operation has long been accepted as a method for promoting EU action. The 1985 Schengen agreement on the abolition of passport controls between five EU member states is an early example of initiatives being taken by member states that valued action over uniformity. It is especially noteworthy that this initiative has cumulatively attracted more adherents. The great majority of EU member states have now adopted the Schengen principles.

The Eurozone was launched through enhanced co-operation with a dozen countries qualified for membership. The integrationist goal of expanding membership led to the prompt admission of countries that have subsequently shown themselves unable to live up to the ECB's standards. In monetary policy the EU is now divided into five different groups of countries: those that currently belong to the Eurozone and meet its standards; those that belong but do not meet its standards; new member states obligated to join the Eurozone as and when they decide that their national finances make this appropriate; countries that have the right to remain outside the Eurozone; and a fifth category that is logically possible but currently without any members, countries that are temporarily or permanently ex-members of the Eurozone.

Enhanced co-operation reverses the priority given the EU's twin principles of unity and diversity; for that reason, Article 20 of the Treaty on the European Union declares that it 'shall be adopted by the Council as a last resort'. It accepts more diversity as a price worth paying to allow more unity among states that want to act together. When the alternative to enhanced co-operation is a few states preventing a majority from co-operating, there is a pragmatic incentive to find ways by which each group can secure what it wants. The commitment to an ever closer Union is not abandoned. It is modified to apply, in the first instance, to those countries that are ready to adopt a policy that requires further integration.

The rhetorical claim that enhanced co-operation threatens the disintegration of the European Union is misleading. Finessing obstacles to consensus through enhanced co-operation means no more and no less than that the involvement of member states differs within a specific and limited policy area. The generations of commitments already embedded in the *acquis communautaire* are not altered.

To describe enhanced co-operation as a form of policy *a la carte* is correct, since member states are free to endorse or reject a proposal. It contrasts with the current policymaking process in which the Commission offers a set menu to member states to consume and negotiates alterations in the set menu. Each member state is expected to accept the same meal, whether this is a policy that it regards as appetizing or difficult to digest. In fact, the appetites of member states for European integration differ. For example, the United Kingdom is keen to see the European Union adopt rules that will increase trade in the single Europe market while opposing rules that regulate how employers produce the goods and services that are traded.

Differentiated integration, the consequence of enhanced co-operation, leads to a messier and looser combination of policy jurisdictions than one-size-fits-all policymaking. If political integration is the primary goal of major EU policies, then any departure from uniformity is undesirable. But tidiness becomes counterproductive when it stifles responses to strong pressures for collective action because of disagreement about what to do. If European integration is valued pragmatically, then any step that can immediately be taken is preferable to standing still. This was, after all, the basis on which the European Union was founded without the participation of what was then Europe's strongest economy and oldest democratic political system, the United Kingdom.

III Bringing in Europe's Citizens

Whatever leaders decide at an EU meeting, they still need followers. It hardly profits policymakers to gain the consent of the European Council and lose the support of Europe's citizens. Within the EU framework, the endorsement of policies by a Council of national governments and a popularly elected European Parliament provides institutional legitimacy. However, it cannot deliver popular commitment. Nor does the opportunity for Europeans to vote once every five years to elect national representatives to a multi-national European Parliament give citizens effective sanctions to hold EU policymakers accountable.

Most citizens see their national government as the institution that ought to do something about the problems that concern them, whether the problem is domestic, European, or global. When the European Election Study asked how much responsibility each level of government had for major problems of interdependence—the economy, immigration, interest rates, and climate change—in all four areas greater responsibility was attributed to the national government than to the European Union. The only difference was the degree to which national governments were more responsible. Furthermore, when people were asked whether the European Union or their national government ought to deal with what respondents regarded as the most important political problem, only one-third named the EU as their preferred policymaker, while two-thirds wanted their national or regional government to deal with it.

Agreements that national governments make at European meetings must be approved and implemented by national parliaments. It is unrealistic to expect Britons, Germans, or Greeks to give passive consent to whatever is decided in Brussels when they can hold their government accountable in their capacity as national citizens. National governors cannot win popular commitment to EU agreements by telling voters they are bound to accept measures because of international treaties signed in the previous century by their long-dead prede-cessors. Neither Angela Merkel nor Francois Hollande had been born when the foundation stone of today's EU, the European Coal and Steel Community, was laid in 1951. Moreover, their position as sole national representative in the European Council exaggerates the backing they have at home. Merkel became the head of a coalition German government after the Christian Democratic Union won just one-third of the German vote in 2009. In 2012 Hollande became French president after winning under 29 per cent of the first-round French vote and then scraping home with 51 per cent of the vote in the second-round ballot.

Referendums as a test of popular commitment to major EU policies. How the European Union develops in future depends on how much popular commitment can be mobilized from people who are both national and European citizens as well as on what is decided in Brussels. To adopt policies without popular commitment makes them vulnerable to evasion or repudiation, especially when the costs create a number of visible losers as well as winners. To be sustainable, major steps towards an ever closer Union require the commitment of losers as well as winners. How can this be achieved?

The most authoritative way to confirm the commitment of Europe's citizens to an ever closer Union is to put a treaty to a pan-European referendum in which all of Europe's citizens have the right to vote. Doing so would give fresh significance to the Lisbon Treaty's principle of taking decisions 'as openly and as closely as possible to the citizen'. A referendum is, by definition, a very open political activity. A pan-European referendum would create a ballot that offers the same choice to every European citizen about a European issue. It would thereby lead to a Europe-wide campaign in which national politicians would have to address European issues. It thus contrasts with a European Parliament election in which voters have 27 different sets of choices about which national party they would like to represent them.

A pan-European referendum would avoid the charade of the European Citizens' Initiative in which civil society organizations could draft the text of a proposal while the Commission need take no action on it. In a referendum on an EU treaty, the text would, as at present, be drafted in Brussels, debated by an intergovernmental conference of member states, and require endorsement by the European Council and the European Parliament. This would pre-commit the great majority of national governments to give it their support in a referendum ballot. Europe's citizens would then vote for or against what is on offer.

A referendum is an institution for making decisions about policies. It gives citizens a chance to register their views without having them filtered through intermediary Party Groups in the European Parliament and governments meeting in the European Council. It thus avoids inferring policy preferences from the votes people cast for parties whose programmes they partly agree with and partly disagree with, especially on the issue of European integration (see Figure 6.3). It also avoids assuming that unanimous endorsement of integration by national governments representing only half their country's voters reflects the actual division of opinion among Europe's citizens.

A pan-European referendum involving all 27 member states would be fairer than the current practice of allowing one or two countries to hold referendums while up to 99 per cent of Europe's citizens have no chance to register their view (see Figure 5.1). Unlike the dozens of measures that the EU adopts each week, European treaties are major changes in the constitution of Europe. A referendum on an EU treaty would be consistent with the practice in many democracies of holding referendums on changes in their national constitution. Unlike a national referendum on joining the European Union, a referendum on increasing EU powers would not pose a drastic In/Out choice concerning EU membership. Because a pan-European referendum would be about conferring new powers on the European Union, it would leave the existing *acquis* intact. If the outcome was positive, it would validate agreements arrived at in Brussels by showing that they were also agreeable to Europe's citizens. If a Treaty was rejected, it would show the need of the horizontal checks and balances operating within Brussels to be complemented by a vertical check in the hands of citizens.

In anticipation of a referendum, discussions about adopting treaties could not proceed as before, because politicians and technocrats could not ignore the elephant of public opinion that would render the final verdict on their work. The claims of national politicians to speak for all their citizens would be moderated by the prospect of having to put their claims to a public test. When deliberating about proposals within the multi-national European Council, national governments would have to ask themselves whether they would be prepared to defend what is proposed before their own citizens. This does not mean that a government's position could or should be dictated by opinion polls, for many points in a treaty are of no interest to ordinary voters and many voters are undecided in their views. The requirement of a pan-European referendum does ensure that those who sign binding treaties on behalf of their citizens would have to explain publicly and subject to challenge why they have done so.

It is a mistake to regard Europe's citizens as polarized into groups strongly for and against European integration (cf. Figure 2.2). Instead, there is a substantial group of open-minded people who take their country's membership in the European Union for granted but do not automatically assume that whatever gives more powers to the European Union is desirable. Indifference or hesitancy about the EU is not a sign of principled opposition to further integration, but of an inclination to make a pragmatic judgement on a proposal. Thus, an individual can favour some measures that would increase integration, for example, protection of the environment, while opposing others, for example, pledging their country to guarantee large sums to bail out governments in Eurozone countries that have run up more debts than they can easily repay.

A European referendum would trigger a campaign in which treaties could be examined by both advocates and critics of what the EU proposes to do. Whereas the election of MEPs in national constituencies focuses on national party choices, a pan-European referendum would focus attention on a single treaty common to all countries. A national leader who had endorsed a treaty in the European Council could justify doing so by invoking national interests. However, media would be alert for contradictions in the way in which a treaty was justified in different national contexts. People who are viewed as European leaders in Brussels could demonstrate their leadership by campaigning not only in their home country but also in other EU countries. Moreover, instead of campaigning in the 'trust me' style of a Tony Blair, as is now common among personalistic party leaders, prominent European politicians would have to campaign on the substantive content of a treaty.

The campaigning that accompanies a national referendum on an EU issue usually raises turnout well above that for a European Parliament election. Referendums also raise the level of information that citizens have about the European Union. National referendums on Europe have shown that most of the time citizens approve of the treaty that their leaders have agreed in Brussels. Whether this happens depends on how much the contents of a treaty appeal when subject to scrutiny during a campaign. The most thorough study of voting in national referendums on EU issues concludes: 'Knowledge about the EU does not necessarily guarantee a positive vote in referendums on EU questions'.[3]

Responding to the views of citizens. Every referendum reveals that the electorate is divided. Popular divisions challenge the EU preference for having treaties endorsed by a consensus. Nonetheless, the expression of differences of opinion is what distinguishes a democratic referendum from an undemocratic plebiscite that unquestioningly approves what leaders want to do.

A basic premise of a democratic vote is that losers as well as winners should accept the outcome. If past patterns persist, most EU referendums would show a majority of countries in favour of further integration and an ever closer Union. A small number of countries would probably favour rejection. A treaty endorsed by a majority of voters and countries would have a far better claim to popular commitment than the Eurozone Economic Stability Treaty that sets out rules limiting what national parliaments can and cannot do in their national budgets. Likewise, a treaty that could not gain support from most of Europe's citizens should force EU policymakers to ask themselves why they are so out of touch with the citizens whom they are meant to represent.

National constitutional amendments normally require approval by a concurring majority, that is, by two or more different institutions or by two or more different methods of calculating approval. In Germany, for example, an amendment must be endorsed by a super-majority of two-thirds voting in the

Bundestag and in the *Bundesrat*. In the United States federal system, an amendment must be approved by a two-thirds vote of both houses of Congress and by three-quarters of state legislatures. The European Union's co-decision process requires ordinary legislation to be approved by an absolute majority in the European Parliament and a super-majority in the Council.

The logic of a concurring majority is easy to explain and defend to people who have dual citizenship. It recognizes that votes would be counted at the national level before being aggregated to show the overall distribution of votes among Europe's citizens. An appropriate formula for approval of a new treaty is that it should be endorsed by a majority of both voters and states. Requiring endorsement by a majority of states would protect small countries from being outvoted by the Union's four most populous countries. Requiring endorsement by a majority of European voters would prevent the EU's many small countries from combining against the majority of Europe's citizens. If a Qualified Majority Vote of two-thirds of states were required for approval, this would demonstrate widespread commitment without raising a great barrier to approval. A large minority of citizens and states would oppose a treaty only if many national governments had grossly misrepresented their citizens at the European level.

Enhanced co-operation provides a mechanism for resolving rather than repressing national divisions. In the majority of countries where a referendum showed popular commitment to a treaty, national governments could go ahead. Making a referendum advisory provides a safety valve in the event that there is an awkward outcome. A national government whose electorate had very narrowly advised rejection could seek minor alterations in a treaty in order to make it nationally acceptable. In the small number of countries where there was a clear majority against a treaty, national governments should be able to invoke a carefully designed opt out clause.

The immediate effect of advancing integration through enhanced co-operation would be to deepen and loosen the Union. The differences between member states are described by a variety of metaphors. The term two-speed Europe is misleadingly deterministic, for it implies that the only difference between member states is in the speed at which they move towards an ever closer Union. In fact, some national governments may question whether the Union today is heading in the right direction. To describe enhanced co-operation as dividing the EU into core countries and a periphery ignores the fact that any differentiation about new powers would initially be minor compared to the scope of the *acquis*. Moreover, the metaphor mistakenly assumes that states are always part of the core or of the periphery. In fact, many countries float between these categories, for example, being part of the Eurozone core but outside the defence core, as is the case with Austria and Finland, or inside the Schengen core but outside the euro core, as is the case with Sweden. If a metaphor is required, a Europe of interlocking rings is more appropriate. Each ring can represent an area of policy integrating different combinations of member states. The internationalization of interdependence means that many rings ought to include countries and institutions on other continents too (see Table 8.1).

The dynamic implication of enhanced co-operation depends on whether divisions are temporary or permanent. The official glossary of the European Union mistakenly describes the variable geometry that results from enhanced co-operation as reflecting 'irreconcilable' differences separating member states.[4] However, insofar as enhanced co-operation differentiates leaders and laggards, then divisions are temporary; some take the lead in testing a new policy, while others watch from the sidelines. If enhanced co-operation appears successful, then laggards can catch up by joining the pioneers, and what originally appeared to be a two-speed Europe becomes a Union in which all member states move together. Catching up describes how Britain became an EU member state after initially refusing to be a founder member. The dynamics of a leaders-and-laggards process is best described as a sooner-or-later movement towards an ever closer Union.

Alternatively, experience may cause a national government to re-affirm its initial decision to avoid commitment to a new policy launched by countries in the vanguard of enhanced co-operation. When the Eurozone was created, the British government adopted a wait-and-see policy and experience has produced a consensus that it is better off out of the Eurozone than in it. The attraction of being outside the Eurozone has also gained strength, albeit for different reasons, in Germany and in Greece. However, whatever their regrets about being in the Eurozone, neither country can avoid the consequences of what their predecessors signed up to.

In a world of interdependence it is unrealistic for any European country to claim that it has the unilateral power to make policies that effectively determine its economic conditions and security. The deepening, broadening, and enlargement of the European Union over more than half a century shows that national governments have no illusion about the limits to their capacity to act alone. In coping with interdependence, each EU member state has a portfolio of commitments, some with the European Union, some with a different combination of European countries, and some with countries and institutions on other continents. The twenty-first century question facing the peoples and governments of Europe is not whether they can go it alone in a world of interdependence. It is how and with whom to co-operate in a world in which no country or continent is an island unto itself.

Further Reading

Because the book is addressed to a public policy audience, I assume readers will want fresh thoughts rather than just a recapitulation of what others have written. In any case, in a Europe in flux going over much that was written before enlargement and before the Eurozone turned out to be different than promised does not take into account the current condition of the European Union. Because this book covers a lot of ground, it necessarily draws on a wide range of sources. This note points interested readers to studies that offer more detail and evidence than a short book can provide.

Among textbooks a good place for a beginner to start is Neil Nugent's *Government and Politics of the European Union* (7th edition, Palgrave Macmillan, 2010); it provides a clear and detailed exposition of the EU's institutions and policies and a good index. *Policy-Making in the European Union*, edited by Helen Wallace, Mark Pollack, and Alasdair Young (6th edition, Oxford University Press, 2010) contains narrative chapters by experts in their respective fields. *The Political System of the European Union* by Simon Hix and Bjorn Hoyland (3rd edition, Palgrave Macmillan, 2011) has lots of political science concepts and quantitative data, especially about the European Parliament.

Because the problems that this book addresses are the accumulation of decisions taken a half a century ago in different contexts, history provides a foundation for understanding contemporary events. Jean Monnet's *Memoirs* (Collins, 1978) gives his account of organizing a replacement for the institutions that had misgoverned him since his birth in 1888. My comparative analysis, *What Is Europe?* (Harper Collins Longman, 1996) emphasizes the transformation of Europe from a league of undemocratic multi-national empires to a Union of nation-states. Desmond Dinan's *Ever Closer Union* (4th edition, Palgrave Macmillan, 2010) is a research-based overview of the development of the EU.

The thematic chapters of *Debates about European Integration*, edited by Mette Eilstrup-Sangiovanni (Palgrave Macmillan, 2006) provide extracts of important texts. *European Integration Theory*, edited by Antje Wiener and Thomas Diez (2nd edition, Oxford University Press, 2009), carefully reviews theories about the European Union and its dynamics. Other overviews of research can be found in *Research Agendas in EU Studies: Stalking the Elephant*, edited by

Michelle Egan, Neil Nugent, and William E. Paterson (Palgrave Macmillan, 2010), and Erik Jones, Anand Menon, and Stephen Weatherill, *The Oxford Handbook of the European Union* (Oxford University Press, 2012).

The European Union system did not exist when the classic literature about representation was written and survey-based literature about representation was founded on a simple American paradigm of voters electing members from single-member Congressional districts. While the European Parliament cannot represent half a billion citizens as well as a national Parliament, its contemporary importance in the EU co-decision system makes it an important institution. *The European Parliament* by three experienced officials of the Parliament, Richard Corbett, Francis Jacobs, and Michael Shackleton, is clear and informative about how it works (8th edition, John Harper, 2011).

European Societies: Mapping Structure and Change by Steffen Mau and Roland Verwiebe (Policy Press, 2010, and previously in German) is a conceptually clear and quantitatively rich source of information about social, economic, and cultural characteristics of the societies of member states. The yearbook of Eurostat, *Europe in Figures* (Luxembourg, European Commission, annual), includes discussions of the data as well as many tables.

The starting point on the web for accessing official and abundant information about the European Union is <http://www.europa.eu>. A detailed and up to date guide to the institutions discussed herein can be found at <http://www.europa.eu/institutions-bodies/ index_en.htm>. The information is also available in the EU's other 22 official languages. Recognizing that the vocabulary in everyday use in Brussels has meanings not normally found in the dictionaries of the languages of member states, the EU provides a guide to its own jargon: <http://www.europa.eu/abc/jargon/index_en.htm>. The results of the latest and past Eurobarometer surveys can be found at <http://www.ec.europa.eu/public_opinion>.

Each of the leading journals in the field—the *Journal of Common Market Studies*, the *Journal of European Public Policy, European Union Politics,* and the *Journal of European Union Integration*—has a website with full search facilities.

A detailed list of my own and associates' specialist publications on Europe can be found in my CV and in the Europe section of the website of the Centre for the Study of Public Policy, <http://www.cspp.strath.ac.uk>.

Endnotes

Introduction

1. For convenience, the term European Union is used to refer to institutions that have operated under different names since the launch of the European Coal and Steel Community in 1951. The term 'Brussels' colloquially refers to the complex of EU institutions sited there and, to a lesser extent, in Luxembourg and Strasbourg.
2. Quoted in Giandomenico Majone, *Dilemmas of European Integration* (Oxford: Oxford University Press, 2005), p. 5. Whether Monnet actually used the term 'stealth' is unclear. What is clear is that he achieved success through his skill of behind-the-scenes networking with national leaders in Bonn, Paris, and Washington. Only in London were his contacts of no avail in gaining support for building a new Europe.
3. See Leon Lindberg and Stuart Scheingold, *Europe's Wouldbe Polity* (Englewood Cliffs, NJ: Prentice-Hall, 1970), p. 41.
4. Quoted from Barroso's annual State of the Union address to the European Parliament, 12 September 2012.
5. See Flash Eurobarometer 294 (2010) and Special Eurobarometer 379 (2011) at <http://www.ec.europa.eu/public_opinion>.
6. Mette Jolly, *The European Union and Its People* (Oxford: Oxford University Press, 2007), p. 245.
7. Herman van Rompuy, 25 May 2010.
8. For my own reservations about the Eurozone at the time it was launched, see Richard Rose, 'Putting Monetary Policy in its Political Place', *Journal of Public Policy*, 22, 2, 2002, pp. 257–69, and other contributions to this special issue that I edited with Michael Artis on currency interdependence inside and outside the Eurozone.
9. Paul Craig, 'The Stability, Coordination and Governance Treaty: Principle, Politics and Pragmatism', *European Law Review*, 37, 3, 2012, p. 248.
10. Quoted in Michael Steen, 'ECB Delves into Messy World of Supervision', *Financial Times*, 13 September 2012.

Chapter 1

1. Hannah Pitkin, *The Concept of Representation* (Berkeley: University of California Press, 1967), p. 2.
2. Robert Dahl, *Democracy and its Critics* (New Haven: Yale University Press, 1989), p. 113.
3. This body is now formally called the Council of the European Union. To avoid confusion with the European Council, in this book it is referred to by its former

name, the Council of Ministers. It is not linked to the Council of Europe in Strasbourg, which was founded in 1949 as an intergovernmental forum without the powers of EU institutions. That Council has more member states than the EU, for example, Russia is among its members.

4. Quoted in Jarle Trondal, *An Emergent European Executive Order* (Oxford: Oxford University Press, 2010), p. 6.
5. Quoted in Mark Bovens, Deirdre Curtin, and Paul 't Hart, eds., *The Real World of EU Accountability: What Deficit?* (Oxford: Oxford University Press, 2010), p. 188.
6. See Javier Arrigui and Robert Thomson, 'States' Bargaining Success in the European Union', *Journal of European Public Policy*, 16, 5, 2009.
7. Quoted by Dorothee Heisenberg, 'The Institution of "Consensus" in the European Union', *European Journal of Political Research*, 44, 1, 2005, p. 82.

Chapter 2

1. Quoted in Rodney Leach, *Europe: A Concise Encyclopedia* (London: Profile Books, 1998), p. 56.
2. Peter Hennessy, *Never Again: Britain, 1945–1951* (London: Jonathan Cape, 1992).
3. Ernst Haas, *The Uniting of Europe* (Stanford: Stanford University Press, 1958), p. 456.
4. See Ian Down and Carole J. Wilson, 'From "Permissive Consensus" to "Constraining Dissensus": a Polarizing Union?', *Acta Politica*, 43, 1, 2008, 26–49.
5. Leon Lindberg and Stuart A. Scheingold, *Europe's Wouldbe Polity* (Englewood Cliffs, NJ: Prentice-Hall, 1970).
6. Aaron Wildavsky, *Speaking Truth to Power: The Art and Craft of Policy Analysis* (Boston: Little, Brown, 1979).

Chapter 3

1. J. Hughes, G. Sasse, and C. Gordon, *Europeanization and Regionalization in the EU's Enlargement to Central and Eastern Europe: The Myth of Conditionality* (Basingstoke: Palgrave Macmillan, 2004), p. 164.
2. See Richard Rose and Kenneth Newton, *Evaluating the Quality of Society and Public Services* (Dublin: European Foundation for Living and Working Conditions, 2010), chapter 7.

Chapter 4

1. *EU Citizenship Report 2010*. Brussels: European Commission, Com 603, 2010.
2. Quoted by Imogen Sudbery, 'Bridging the Legitimacy Gap in the EU: Can Civil Society Bring the Union Closer to its Citizens?', *Collegium*, 26, 2003, p. 90.
3. Beate Kohler-Koch, 'Civil Society and EU Democracy: "Astroturf" Representation?', *Journal of European Public Policy*, 17, 1, 2010, p. 111.
4. Jan W. van Deth, 'The "Good European Citizen"', *European Political Science*, 8, 2009, pp. 175–89.

5. *The White Paper on Multi-Level Governance* (Brussels: Committee of the Regions, 2009), p. 11.
6. For a detailed discussion of the Convention, see D. Castiglione, J. Schoenlau, C. Longman, E. Lombardo, N. Borragan, and M. Aziz, *Constitutional Politics in the European Union* (Basingstoke: Palgrave Macmillan, 2007).

Chapter 5

1. 'A Post-Functionalist Theory of European Integration', *British Journal of Political Science*, 39, 1, 2009, p. 20.
2. Jean Monnet, *Memoirs* (London: Collins, 1978), p. 367.
3. Jean-Claude Piris, *The Lisbon Treaty* (Cambridge: Cambridge University Press, 2010), p. 50.
4. <http://www.EUprofiler.eu>.
5. Quoted in Sara Binzer Hobolt, *Europe in Question* (Oxford: Oxford University Press, 2009), p. 23.
6. See the results of the 2004 International Social Science Programme survey cited by Shaun Bowler, Todd Donovan, and Jeffery Karp, 'Enraged or Engaged? Preferences for Direct Citizen Participation in Affluent Democracies', *Political Research Quarterly*, 60, 3, 2007, p. 352.

Chapter 6

1. Richard Corbett, Francis Jacobs, and Michael Shackleton, *The European Parliament* (London: John Harper, 8th edition, 2011), p. 3.
2. Berthold Rittberger, *Building Europe's Parliament* (Oxford: Oxford University Press, 2005), p. 106.
3. Martin Westlake, *A Modern Guide to the European Parliament* (London: Pinter, 1994), p. 17.
4. *Draft Report on a Proposal for a Modification of the Act Concerning the Election of the Members of the European Parliament* (Brussels: European Parliament 2010/XXXX(INI) 12 April 2010), p. 39.
5. All statistics refer to the European Parliament elected in 2009 with 736 MEPs. The implementation of the Lisbon Treaty added a small number of additional seats and on admission to the EU in summer 2013 Croatia will receive seats. This will force a redistribution of seats for the Parliament elected in 2014.
6. The percentages are taken from a survey of 171 members of the European Parliament conducted by David Farrell, Simon Hix, and Roger Scully in 2010.

Chapter 7

1. For full details, see Richard Rose and Gabriela Borz, 'Aggregation and Representation in European Parliament Party Groups', *West European Politics*, forthcoming, 2013, and Borz and Rose, 'Mapping Parties across Europe with EU Profiler Data', *CSPP Studies in Public Policy*, 470, 2010.

2. See results of the 2009 European Election Survey.

3. These percentages are taken from a survey of 171 members of the European Parliament conducted by David Farrell, Simon Hix, and Roger Scully in 2010.

Chapter 8

1. Norwegian Ministry of Foreign Affairs, *Outside and Inside: Norway's Agreements with the European Union* (Oslo: Official Norwegian Reports NOU, 2012), p. 6.

2. Steffen Mau and Roland Verwiebe, *European Societies: Mapping Structure and Change* (Bristol: Policy Press, 2010), p. 344.

3. Richard Rose and Kenneth Newton, *Evaluating the Quality of Society and Public Services in Europe* (Dublin: European Foundation for Living and Working Conditions, 2010), pp. 44ff.

Chapter 9

1. See *Transatlantic Trends*, June 2012, a project of the German Marshall Fund.

2. For details, see Jean-Claude Piris, *The Future of Europe: Towards a Two-Speed EU?* (Cambridge: University Press, 2012).

3. Sara Binzer Hobolt, *Europe in Question*, p. 107.

4. See <http://www.europa.eu/legislation_summaries/glossary/>.

Index